The Web Factory
guide to
Marketing
on the
Internet

About the Author

Anna Ollier graduated from Swansea University in 1992 with a degree in business and languages, specialising in marketing and consumer behaviour. Anna began her career in the field of the environment, working for an environmental policy charity. She specialised in corporate fundraising and corporate environmental reporting on the Internet, and has worked with several large UK companies advising them on their corporate environmental reporting strategy on the Internet. She was also invited to judge the 1997 International Water Services Association Public Relations Internet Award. In 1995 she set up her own consultancy developing courseware and training specialised Internet courses, particularly in the voluntary sector, including a course on Marketing on the Internet. Anna has also been designing, creating and maintaining Web pages for voluntary sector organisations and small businesses for 3 years, and advising on Internet strategy.

Acknowledgements
The author wishes to thank Kim Worts of Aurelian Information Ltd for her invaluable support and Elena Rodriguez for her comments.

This book is dedicated to Marie-Louise, Colette and Fabrice

ISBN 1 899247 10 6
Published by Aurelian Information Ltd
129 Leighton Gardens, London NW10 3PS Tel 0181-960 7918
http://www.dircon.co.uk/aurelian

The information in this book is believed to be correct at the time of going to press but must not be treated as a substitute for detailed advice in individual situations. It is published without responsibility on the part of Aurelian Information or the author, whether arising from any negligence, misrepresentation or otherwise for loss occasioned to any person or organisation acting or refraining from acting as a result of any information contained herein.

The Web Factory

guide to

Marketing on the Internet

Anna Ollier

AURELIAN INFORMATION UK

A Word from *The Web Factory*

When approached by Aurelian Information, we were excited at the prospect of sponsoring a publication aimed at describing the steps that companies should adopt in using the Internet as a marketing medium - both for research and promotion. But would it, we asked, give the reader a clear understanding of what's involved in harnessing the awesome power of the Internet and provide an objective view of the steps necessary to implement it into the overall business development strategy?

There is no doubt that the Internet already plays a vital part in many organisations' business strategy. The accelerating global marketplace and customers' desire for rapid, individual and exclusive service puts increasing pressure on organisations to improve performance. For all organisations - both large and small, local, national and international - the Internet represents a whole new and productive way of conducting business day to day, allowing them to seize competitive advantage now and in the future. Effective use of the Internet will result in increased business efficiency, reduced operational costs and improved customer satisfaction.

This book provides an excellent introduction to marketing on the Internet, offering examples and case studies on how to implement an effective marketing or campaigning strategy. The content clearly reflects Anna Ollier's extensive experience in providing training and consultancy for Internet marketing.

As a leading provider of complete Internet and Intranet business solutions, **The Web Factory** is delighted that Anna has written this guide. We trust that by reading it you will be able to grasp the Internet opportunity with confidence.

Contents

The **Internet for All** *Series*

First Steps on the Internet *Sandra Vogel*

Tested by rock-bottom beginners! Everything you need to know to get started on the Internet. Sandra dumps technical jargon and explains each step in plain English - finding what you want on the Web, talking to newsgroups, sending and receiving e-mails, all the wonders of the Internet. 'a brilliant book' *Internet beginner* 'inspiring - welcomes absolute beginners and has a lot to teach old hands' *Total Internet* 'For those who feel left behind in the IT revolution ... hit the ground running' *Circulation*.
ISBN 1 899247 08 4 Price £12.99 (Post free in UK)

Managing Non-profits on the Internet - a guide to strategy

Adrian Lanning with *Malcolm Corbett . Howard Lake . Dominic Search*
A complete overview of the opportunities and threats posed by the Internet. The first book for directors and managers in the non-profits world on evaluating and creating a policy for projects on the Internet and the World Wide Web. How to plan - what to do now, what do tomorrow - and why. How to direct strategy and what to avoid. With sobering advice that applies to profit-seeking organisations, too!
In association with Poptel
ISBN 1 899247 09 2 Price £15.99 (Post free in UK)

Direct Connection's guide to
Fundraising on the Internet *Howard Lake*

The classic book on Internet fundraising by the acknowledged authority on the subject. Howard Lake's widely-praised book shows how the Internet, used at local, national or international level can raise funds, find and keep donors, promote appeals, sell merchandise and speed day-to-day tasks. 'Earth-breaking guide *The Guardian* 'packed with ideas' *Professional Fundraising* 'Thoroughly researched - easy to read - informative - inspirational' *Voluntary Voice*
ISBN 899247 06 8 Price £12.99 (Post free in UK)

Forthcoming titles **Finding Information on the Internet**
Building a Selling Web Site

ORDERS: AURELIAN INFORMATION LIMITED
129 Leighton Gardens   London NW10 3PS
Tel: 0181-960 7918   Fax: 0171-794 8609   E-mail: aurelian@dircon.co.uk

1 Introduction

What is marketing on the Internet?

The Internet has spawned an entirely new way of carrying out marketing activities. It allows organisations to complete the whole marketing cycle in one place. Everything through from market research, product development, distribution, promotion, advertising and selling to customer service and support can now be done on the Internet.

The Internet is evolving at a rapid pace and there are many outstanding issues such as limited bandwidth and secure credit card transactions to be solved before it will become completely market-friendly. It is not a mainstream medium yet but, by exploring opportunities now, organisations will be prepared for the new marketing model of the future.

The aim of this book is to explain clearly how marketing and campaigning professionals can make the best use of the Internet. It provides examples and case studies of good practice and success stories as well as sound guidelines on how to implement an effective marketing or campaigning strategy on the Internet.

Key Internet marketing facilities

Marketing on the Internet describes all the marketing-related activities, such as advertising and selling, that are carried out on the World Wide Web, through Newsgroups, mailing lists and via e-mail.

Although the Internet in its broadest terms encompasses all the above, and more, the Web is the part of the Internet that is most widely used for marketing activities. This book therefore focuses primarily on the opportunities offered by the Web.

How does it compare with off-line marketing?

The Internet provides a unique medium for marketing. It has created new ways of targeting and informing customers and a new approach to the marketing mix.

The buzzwords of marketing on the Internet are 'one to one marketing' - where marketers can market to the individual's needs - 'value added marketing' - offering something of value such as entertainment or information, in return for consumer's attention to the marketing message, and 'stakeholder dialogue' - or relationship marketing, where marketers engage consumers in a continuing dialogue which translates into repeat visits to the Web site and customer loyalty.

This book reveals how Internet marketing can take you to places that are undreamed of by traditional marketing methods.

The Internet has unique attributes - setting it quite apart in many respects from traditional marketing media. It is interactive, non-linear, unobtrusive. Consumers pull information rather than have the message pushed at them as in traditional media. The consumer has control over processing information and this remains available as a permanent record. The Internet is transactional and can display audio, video and multimedia.

The Internet creates the opportunity to reach a global audience at a fraction of the cost of traditional marketing channels and at the same time it enables organisations to reach a fine-tuned level of market segmentation. The Internet also facilitates customised content, enabling you to offer personalised marketing messages.

Throughout this book you will learn how to make the most of the Internet's unique features to communicate your marketing message in differing contexts.

Many of the traditional marketing channels are being eroded by the Internet and replaced by new models. Distribution channels are becoming shorter and marketers are now faced with communicating directly with consumers via the Web, cutting out distributors. This 'disintermediation' of distribution channels is opening up new responsibilities for marketers. New ways of marketing mean that marketers must familiarise themselves with a new marketing paradigm and learn new skills, identify new opportunities - or get left behind.

This book will help you to identify which new options you should be considering and what precisely are the resources necessary to take them to completion.

It is very easy to get carried away with your Internet marketing strategy and dismiss traditional marketing methods which may, in fact, be more appropriate for your organisation or product. The Internet is not appropriate for every marketing activity or every organisation. The present book shows where Internet marketing *is* appropriate and how to integrate your on-line and off-line strategies.

Summary

O   The Internet can assist marketers with market research, product development, distribution, promotion, advertising, selling and customer service and support.

O   The Web is the part of the Internet that is most widely used for marketing activities.

O   The Internet is changing the nature of marketing and has created new opportunities for marketers including personalised marketing messages, value added marketing and relationship marketing.

O   Marketing on the Internet is quite different from traditional marketing.

O   The Internet is not appropriate for every marketing activity or every organisation.

2 The First Steps

The first steps before implementing a marketing strategy on the Internet involve:

O   determining whether the Internet is an appropriate marketing medium for your organisation

O   determining whether your target market can be reached via the Internet and what their needs are

O   setting realistic marketing objectives for your organisation on the Internet.

Is the Internet an appropriate marketing medium for your organisation?

The Internet can provide new and exciting ways to market your products or services as well as offer the opportunity to create new products and services. But before launching into an Internet marketing strategy it is important to consider carefully whether the medium is appropriate for your organisation's marketing activities.

It is only through careful analysis of the suitability of the medium that you can determine which parts of the marketing mix can be usefully implemented on the Internet.

It may be that the Internet is only appropriate for carrying out certain of your organisation's marketing activities, such as market research, but inappropriate for others, such as selling your products or services.

You will need to familiarise yourself with the characteristics of the medium, its possibilities and its limitations before being able to make an informed decision as to whether it is appropriate for each marketing activity to be considered.

Market Research

Most organisations need information of some sort or another, about competitors, markets or regulatory procedures. The Internet is a mine of information on products, services, individuals and organisations. Perhaps the biggest source of information on the Internet comes from the users themselves who can be accessed by e-mail, Web or Newsgroups. This information can be tapped for market research purposes.

Primary data

The Internet is most appropriate for carrying out primary research where you can identify and communicate with your target market. The Web, in particular, is a useful tool for posting a survey to collect primary data on your audience, such as demographics.

Secondary data

Given the wealth of reports, surveys, statistics and data available on the Internet it is likely that there is something for every marketing professional's needs. The main thing to be aware of here is that information available on the Internet may not always be as reliable as that obtained via traditional methods. The issue of the reliability of information on the Internet is discussed in Chapter 4.

Product development

An important part of marketing is developing and maintaining an effective product mix, including modifying existing products and developing new ones. The Internet can be a low risk and inexpensive way of developing new products or services and carrying out test marketing. Newsgroups are an excellent area to generate new product ideas through discussion and to take products or services through the concept stage.

Products or services that can be delivered over the Internet can also be tested on a global market of potential consumers. Many software products are tested in this way. New software is released in beta versions over the Internet and distributed either via ftp servers or over the Web. Users are invited to try the software free of charge and comment on any improvements that could be made and notify of any bugs.

The Internet itself offers a wealth of opportunities for the creation of new products and services that can *only* exist on the Internet, such as information based products and services, e-zines (electronic magazines) for example.

Product distribution

Some organisations market products or services that are only available via the Internet.

The artist formerly known as Prince *<http://www.love4oneanother.com>* *plans to launch a limited edition four-CD set of tracks previously only available on bootleg, exclusively available on the Web.*

In:sync *<http://www.in-sync.com>* *distributes its digital video editing software Kohesion for Internet content developers, CD ROM designers and Video editors exclusively over the Web. A 30-day evaluation copy is available after which you can purchase a copy on-line if you like it.*

The decision to distribute your product or service over the Internet should be taken in the light of improving the accessibility of your product to the market. Distribution over the Internet is low risk and you can easily change distribution systems if you are not successful. The Internet can be used to distribute both consumer and business/industrial products and services.

If you are considering distributing traditional products or services directly over the Internet you must look at how this will affect your relationship with your regular distributors and retailers.

The traditional marketing channel of producer-wholesaler-retailer-consumer is slowly being eroded and replaced by a new marketing system where producers interface directly with the consumer via the Internet. Traditional retailers should examine how this will affect their business and adapt to the new environment by working on their current strengths, such as their relationships with customers. Producers will need to learn new skills in order to communicate effectively with consumers.

An important part of distribution is order-processing, including order entry, handling and delivery. Order entry can be effected over the Web with the help of interactive forms. Handling depends very much on the degree of integration between your Web server and existing inventory and payment systems.

Many products or services can actually be delivered over the Internet. Software, music, video, pictures and books can all be delivered over the Internet as can services such as on-line advice shops.

Obviously, products or services that can be both sold and delivered direct over the Internet are more appropriate for Internet marketing.

Perhaps one of the most important things to consider when deciding whether to distribute your product or service over the Internet is your ability or willingness to distribute globally. The Internet is worldwide. If you do not wish, or are not able, to fulfil orders from overseas you should spell this out clearly.

If you do wish to distribute worldwide think about whether you have the necessary resources and infrastructure.

Product promotion

Information The Internet lends itself well to providing extensive information about products and services. If your product or service needs large amounts of documentation in order to be understood, the Internet is a cost-effective way of providing this. With the help of search engines and integrated product databases, the Internet provides an appropriate mechanism to deliver customised content that meets consumers needs.

Publicity An effective Internet marketing strategy can generate positive publicity either by winning an award or by being unique. On the other hand if your Internet marketing strategy is not successful, for instance by failing to deliver promised content, be prepared for negative publicity. If you cannot allocate the necessary resources for a successful Internet marketing strategy, then you should think twice about the question of marketing your organisation on the Internet.

Capital FM <http://www.capitalfm.co.uk/> *won the UK Web Awards 1997 Site of the Year Award because of its appeal to a mass market and the way that it has effectively merged its off-line activities with a strong on-line presence. It also uses new technology in the form of real-time streamed audio to broadcast its programmes over the net, offering a unique value-added feature.*

Advertising   The Internet is being hailed as the new advertising medium. New and innovative ways of advertising on the Internet, from Webvertisements to Interstitials (discussed in Chapter 5) are appearing all the time.   However, there are still few reliable methods for identifying and analysing advertising targets on the Internet and evaluating the effectiveness of a campaign.

Organisations should beware of the allure of the relatively low appropriation required for Internet advertising compared to other media. Marketing media planners must approach the decision to advertise on the Internet with the same rigour as for other media vehicles.   Part of a media planner's brief should be to understand and analyse carefully the characteristics of the media as an advertising channel, which are very different from traditional advertising channels.   And then consider whether the Internet is an appropriate way to promote a product, service or organisation.

Selling

Use of the Internet to provide the direct sale of products is still in the experimental stage whilst issues such as electronic payment methods and security are being addressed.   At the other end of the line, businesses are experimenting with selling a variety of products and services over the Internet. Few, though, are asking themselves the question "Is my product or service appropriate for selling over the Internet?".

Chapter 6 gives guidelines on what kinds of products and services are proving the most suitable.

When putting together your strategy it is very important to consider whether you wish to include actual selling on-line or, for example, if you prefer to receive e-mails requesting catalogues or to create leads which will be fulfilled in the traditional way.

Customer service and support

As more and more people have access to the Internet, it is becoming increasingly pertinent for organisations to offer customer support and service at least by e-mail, as customers expect it. Many offer customer support via dedicated Newsgroups or Frequently Asked Questions (FAQ) documents on the Web.

If you are offering on-line purchasing facilities you should investigate what level of on-line support you plan to provide.

For example, the Newsgroup comp.databases.ms-access provides support for the popular database package Microsoft Access.

Products or services that closely match the demographics of the Internet will have greater marketing success than those that do not. So, the next step is to determine whether your target audience can be reached by the Internet and if so, what are their needs?

Internet demographics

Before embarking on an all-out marketing strategy on the Internet it is worth spending some time thinking carefully about whether the medium can reach your target audience.

The very first question should be - is your audience on-line?

Products or services that are targeted at consumers who match the demographic profile of Internet users will achieve greater marketing potential. For example, if your product or service is targeted at computer users - by definition Internet users are computer users - you will have greater marketing success than if they are not.

The average income levels of Internet users are almost double those of non-Internet users, therefore if your product or service appeals to this target market your chances of success are greater.

In some cases the Internet may open up access to previously inaccessible market segments. In other cases it may be that your target audience is amongst a growing percentage of Internet users, such as women and older users.

The Samaritans *started an e-mail counselling service (confidential: samaritans@anon.twwells.com non-confidential: jo@samaritans.org) in the UK in 1996, in response to research that shows that young professional males, a demographic segment that also corresponds to computer users, are particularly at risk of suicide. This group is historically a difficult one to target for* The Samaritans. *However, since the launch of the service they have dealt with thousands of contacts, a high proportion of whom expressed suicidal feelings. They also have a Web site <http://www.samaritans. org.uk> which aims to reach younger people and offer instant contact if they need to talk.*

Internet usage is changing all the time. Your target audience may not currently be on-line but they may be in the near future - it is worth thinking about a possible Internet marketing strategy now and be one step ahead of the game.

Is my target audience on-line?

With 6 million people in Britain accessing the Internet according to National Opinion Poll's *Research Group 1997 UK Internet Survey,* see below, it is quite possible that your target audience is already on-line.

This number is expected to increase by 50% within the next year, so even if your target audience is not currently on-line there is a good chance that they will be very soon.

Reliable statistics on who uses the Internet are difficult to find. Statistics on local, for example UK, users of the Internet, are even harder to find. There are companies who specialise in market research on Internet demographics, but at a price.

There are, however, places on the Internet where you can get some of this information free of charge. These include:

National Opinion Poll's (NOP) *Research Group 1997 UK Internet Survey* *<http://www.nopres.co.uk/index.html>*

This survey reveals that the number of households in Britain with Internet access more than doubled in the twelve months to June 1997.

The survey announced:

O   **That around one in 25 households in Britain are now linked to the Internet; the figure more than doubled from just under 400,000 in June 1996 to 960,000 in June 1997.**

O   **Internet usage for educational purposes increased at the fastest rate with 48% in June 1997 compared to 39% in June 1996.**

O   **Around 6 million adults used the Internet between June 1996 and June 1997, and approx 9 million adults are expected to have used it by June 1998.**

O   **52% of all who used the Web in the last three months declared they were dissatisfied with the speed of downloading pages with graphics - a clear message to all involved in Web design.**

The survey is updated on an annual basis.

Graphics, Visualisation and Usability Centre's WWW *User Surveys* <*http://www.cc.gatech.edu/gvu/user_surveys/*>. *This survey, which is regularly updated, is not fully representative of world-wide usage as US users are over-represented, but it can be used indicatively. The US tends to be about 6 months ahead of the UK in Internet terms.*

Redsquare <*http://www.redsquare.co.uk/question.htm*> *This marketing company is conducting a 1997 UK Internet Survey to provide data specific to the UK's Internet user-base. Results of this survey are updated on the first Monday of each month. In August 1997, the typical profile of a Web user was:*

O   **A single male aged 22-30 who owns his own home and car, lives in or near a metropolitan area and may have an income exceeding £40k pa.**

O   **If he reads a paper, it's likely to be The Guardian - he's well educated (to degree level) and holds a senior position in the banking, finance or business services sectors.**

○ **He's been using the net for a year or more, and uses it every day at work for Web browsing and e-mail, spending more than 5 hours each week on-line.**

NUA Internet *Marketing* *<http://www.nua.ie/surveys/index.cgi>* has a good summary of several Internet user surveys. You can also find details of surveys on Internet use in other countries.

Yahoo at *<http://www.yahoo.com/Computers/Internet/Statistics_and_Demo graphics>* has links to Internet demographic surveys.

Existing stakeholders

You may decide that your first step in marketing on the Internet will be to communicate with existing stakeholders. The advantage of this is that you already have a relationship with them which helps you determine their needs.

An easy way of discovering whether your existing stakeholders are on-line or not is to ask them. A simple questionnaire (perhaps as an addition to another questionnaire being sent out or included in a mailout) would do the trick.

It should cover whether or not they are on-line and, if so, what method they use to access the Internet (useful for determining whether they are low-bandwidth or high-bandwidth users). If they are not currently on-line then the survey should discover whether they are planning to go on-line in the near future. Finally, find out whether they would prefer to be contacted on-line - and, if so, what their e-mail address is.

Potential stakeholders

Once you gain experience in communicating your marketing message to existing stakeholders the next step is to target prospective stakeholders who are on-line.

One common mistake made by marketers is to think of the Internet as some mass communications medium. An effective Internet marketing strategy should attempt to communicate with a well researched and highly targeted part of the Internet.

It is therefore worth spending some time getting to know whether your target audience is on-line.

Global on-line markets

Whilst the Internet is a global phenomenon, not all countries are connected to it, and among those that are, access may be limited. If your existing or prospective stakeholders are in another country, check that country's Internet access and demographics.

What are my audience's needs?

After establishing that your audience is on-line or about to be, the next step is to find out what their Internet needs are.

Alarmingly, research conducted by the **Gartner** group in 1996 <http://www.gartner.com> suggested that 90 percent of business Web sites are not delivering content and services that meet their customers' requirements. As a result, Gartner predicts that 75 percent of Web sites will need to be rewritten or rearchitectured within the first 12 months of operation. The Gartner study shows that users do not want content such as corporate descriptions and press releases. They want useful applications such as advanced interactive technical support and the ability to query databases to get answers to their questions. They want to be able to access product information that specifically meets the needs they define.

Too often, Web sites are company-driven and not customer-driven. A team of marketing professionals, technicians, designers and management gets together and decides what the content of their Web site should be, rather than taking the time to research, understand and meet the needs of the end user.

Large budgets are devoted to researching consumer needs in respect of traditional marketing activities. The same should be true of any Internet marketing activities in order to avoid failure and lack of interest from consumers in response to your efforts to reach them effectively.

In order to understand the requirements of your audience you can:

O   Have your site reviewed by a usability group made up from your intended audience to determine whether it meets their needs and requirements

O   Place a survey at your Web site asking visitors to comment on content

O   Circulate a questionnaire to find out what your target market uses the Internet for, and what kind of information they would like to see from your organisation on the Internet

Now you know whether there is anyone out there to listen to your marketing message and whether what they want to hear is what you are ready to deliver.

Setting realistic marketing objectives

Once you have determined whether it is appropriate to market your product or service on the Internet and whether your target market can be reached via the Internet, the next step is to set clear marketing aims and objectives.

The key to a successful Internet marketing strategy is a focused set of objectives and a targeted set of stakeholders.

Your marketing objectives may be to:

O   raise awareness of your product or service by providing extensive information on it
O   improve distribution of your product or service and increase customer satisfaction
O   increase sales
O   reduce costs
O   improve communications with stakeholders
O   strengthen branding
O   establish your organisation as a cutting-edge, hi-tech innovator
O   improve customer service
O   reach new markets

O   test new products and services
O   improve daily processes and efficiency

Non-profit making organisations may also want to:

O   increase fundraising revenue
O   increase donations of services

A clear set of objectives for your marketing strategy need to obey the following criteria:

O   *be measurable.* For example if the aim is to increase sales by x then sales must be measurable
O   *incorporate a temporal element,* setting a time-frame for accomplishing objectives
O   *be consistent* with your organisation's off-line marketing aims and objectives and with the organisation's overall goals
O   *reflect available resources.* A global fully transactional electronic commerce site on the Web demands specialist skills and resources and you will need to think about the resources needed for handling new international business.

Finally, you must not forget to allocate a budget for your Internet marketing strategy and decide on responsibilities for implementation.

Some of the costs involved will include: training; software and hardware such as Merchant Server software and Web servers; specialist consultancy such as Web designers, programmers and database experts and organisation-wide Internet access, perhaps over a LAN. You should be able to recoup some costs through savings in printing and distribution, perhaps through raising revenue from advertising on your Web site and reducing personnel costs through automating processes over the Internet.

Summary

O   Determine whether the Internet is an appropriate marketing medium for your organisation.

○ The Internet can be used for market research, product development, product distribution, product promotion, selling and customer services and support.

○ Products or services that closely match the demographics of the Internet will have greater marketing success than those that don't.

○ It is worth spending some time determining whether your target market can be reached via the Internet.

○ The Internet can be used to reach new and existing stakeholders.

○ It is important to address your audience's Internet needs to avoid lack of interest in your Internet marketing strategy.

○ The key to a successful Internet marketing strategy is a focused set of objectives which will help you gauge the success of your Internet marketing activities.

○ It is important to set a realistic and comprehensive budget for your Internet marketing activities.

3 Integrating Internet Marketing with Traditional Marketing Methods

An effective Internet marketing strategy must be fully and wholly integrated with your organisation's overall business objectives and firmly placed within your current marketing strategy.

To be effective, Internet marketing must not be seen as a separate and exclusive area of activity - it should operate to amplify and complement your traditional marketing activities as well as initiating new avenues.

For example, you could place a job advert in newspaper classifieds and provide more information on the Web. The Web address should be mentioned in your traditional adverts. It is cheaper to hold information on the Web than to take a large advert in a newspaper.

So, by referring the audience captured by the print advert to the Web you can offer them detailed information on the product they have selected.

An advertisement appeared in a national daily newspaper inviting readers to tap into www.teach.org.uk if they wanted to find out about 'a profession that's://challenging/exciting/intellectually stimulating'. The Web site then contained further details on careers in the teaching profession.

Another print advertisement asks the question 'Should we continue cutting down forests?' And invites readers to access **The Timber Trade Federation** *Web site at <http://www.ttf.co.uk> to find out more.*

Dell *<http://www.dell.co.uk>* *in one of their newspaper advertising campaigns encourages users to visit their Web site 'because [their] prices change to print'. The advert also draws attention to the fact that customers can order on-line 24hrs a day. The advert features one of their products which comes with a free modem if ordered over the Internet.*

In these examples the print advertisement gives just enough information to link it to an organisation or subject which is fully detailed on the Web site. Placing all this information in the print advert would have been costly.

By combining the print medium and the Web, organisations are able to implement a more effective and informative marketing campaign.

The rewards of implementing a well-integrated Internet marketing strategy include:

Communication. Internal networks, known as Intranets (For information on Intranets see Chapter 9) can greatly improve communications between marketing, public relations and sales departments, greatly improving your marketing communications as a whole.

Access to information. Think of the benefits and cost savings of being able to access up-to-date product descriptions and prices on-line from your organisation's Intranet as well as the latest marketing reports on the Internet and use this to improve your traditional marketing activities.

Guidelines to creating a successfully integrated Internet marketing strategy

An Internet marketing strategy takes elements of the traditional marketing mix and uses the Internet to improve their effectiveness and efficiency, eg:

O   **distribution of software can be enhanced by delivery over the Web**
O   **customer services can be improved by providing order tracking over the Web**
O   **publicity for a product can be heightened by stimulating discussion of it in Newsgroups**

Some marketing functions may be replaced by the Internet. For example, the Internet enables direct sales of products and services to be obtained from the producer - bypassing and thereby reducing or even obviating the need for traditional distribution channels - unless the traditional channel leads to a market which cannot be reached via the Internet.

Internet marketing plans and existing marketing plans should be clearly tied in. For example, your Web site should have clear links to the rest of the organisation's marketing strategy eg. if your product positioning strategy is to project an upmarket image you must not then contradict this with a Web site with downmarket appeal.

Your Internet marketing strategy should be explained effectively internally. Companies still have some way to go in communicating and incorporating the strategic benefits of the Internet on an organisation-wide basis. The key is to educate your advertising, communications and public relations staff in the requirements and opportunities for integration with Internet strategies. Obtain board level commitment and understanding of the business benefits of an Internet marketing strategy.

You should know when to stop. In certain cases it may be appropriate to take marketing on the Internet only so far. For example, you may choose to take your marketing strategy as far up the sales chain as possible but choose to stop short at actual product ordering and selling, relying instead on traditional methods such as faxing an order form and paying over the phone. This could be because either your organisation's infrastructure or your target market is not ready for buying and selling over the Internet.

Restructure your corporate communications (Business cards, Annual Reports, Press releases, Corporate letterhead) to reflect your Internet presence. Internet information should be made mandatory on all corporate literature and could be included on your corporate vehicle fleet, product packaging and promotional items, such as pens. Traditional direct marketing tools such as the telephone, fax and mail should also refer to your Internet marketing activities.

Ensure that you have access to the right balance of skills to do the job. A full skills audit should be carried out to ascertain in-house expertise and identify gaps to be filled by training or outsourcing. There is little point in setting up an Intranet to keep your sales force up-to-date with the latest product specifications and prices if they have not been trained in how to use it.

Know when it is appropriate to combine traditional marketing expertise with Internet experts. Traditional marketers can benefit from working with Internet specialists on the team. For example, the Levi's site was created by US On-line specialist Organic On-line, working with their advertising agency Foote Cone Belding, UK Web specialist Obsolete and UK advertising agency Bartle Bogle Hegarty.

Make sure that your Web site is supported by adequate organisational resources. An obvious example: if one of the main objectives of your site is to increase sales, make plans to deal with increased demand and consider increasing your sales force.

There are similarities between traditional and on-line marketing. For instance, conducting on-line focus groups - these can follow the same format as traditional focus groups. But there are just as many differences which require different approaches and mindsets, such as promotional interactive Web sites. See Chapter 7 on building a marketing Web site.

Remember, there are no boundaries on the Internet. Be careful to avoid undermining your traditional marketing strategy and alienating your regular markets and distributors by, for example, implementing differential pricing strategies for on-line and off-line markets.

Do not neglect markets that do not have Internet access. It is very easy to forget or alienate your traditional audience by excluding them from your marketing strategy.

You could, for instance, copy your Web site to a CD-ROM, bundle it with a Web browser and send this to stakeholders who do not have access to the Internet.

CD-ROMS and the Internet

One of the major current limitations of the Internet is the lack of available bandwidth, which makes it very difficult to deliver truly multimedia content over the Web. CD-ROMS on the other hand are limited by no such thing and can, in fact, store large quantities of data. Perfect for multimedia files. CD-ROMS can also be linked to the Internet. You could create a link from a CD-ROM to your Web site and from there have other links.

Dorling Kindersley publishers <http://www.dk.com/> for example has dedicated sites for some of its titles - only accessible via the disc. The Web sites are like magazines and are not linked to the rest of the Web.

CD-ROMS are also ideal for storing the bandwidth-hungry multimedia elements of a Web site. This approach is very useful for storing information that is static and then linking it to the Web which contains dynamic data such as prices and availability. New technology means that CD-ROMS can interface seamlessly with the Web giving the impression that content is continuously changing.

Summary

O   A successful Internet marketing strategy is one that is
     integrated with your traditional marketing activities.
O   Some marketing functions such as distribution can be
     replaced by the Internet.
O   There are just as many similarities as differences between
     Internet marketing and traditional marketing. It is
     important to understand these.
O   The integration of CD-ROMS with the Web is a good
     example of how 'traditional' and Internet marketing media
     can complement and enhance each other.

4 Market Research on the Internet

Information is power. Organisations need all kinds of marketing information to improve the marketer's ability to make decisions and guarantee marketing success. They can use the Internet to gain competitive advantage by improving their marketing information systems and market research strategies.

The Internet can be used to conduct primary and secondary research - both quantitative and qualitative.

In particular, it can be used to:

○ *Collect demographics* and psychographics
○ *Research and identify target markets*, for example, regional markets
○ *Try out new ideas and test consumer response to new products.* Software companies are doing this by providing demo versions of their software on their Web sites and compiling lists of potential customers for the finished product
○ *Access information about competitors'* products and services
○ *Obtain instant feedback on the likes and dislikes of customers*, suggestions for improvement and potential problems. By taking on board customers' comments, organisations can deliver products and services that truly meet customers' requirements.
○ *Obtain feedback on your Web site* - whether they like your site or not and how you might improve design, layout and content.

The benefits of conducting marketing research on the Internet include:

○ **The ability to survey much wider audiences more cheaply than through traditional methods. Cost savings can be made on travel expenses for focus groups, telephone costs for telephone interviews and printing and distribution costs for mail surveys. In addition, because Internet research is largely automated there are cost savings to be made on hiring personnel for interviewing and data entry such as those required in traditional market surveys**

○ **Information can be obtained 24 hours a day, every day**

○ **Surveys on the Web can easily be changed or added to at no extra cost**

○ **Data can be very quickly converted into a database or statistical package making it instantly available for reporting**

○ **Increasing sample sizes has a marginal impact on cost relative to the cost of increasing sample sizes for traditional methods**

However, whilst Internet users are growing and are now an important component of many firms' target market, the demographics of the Internet are still fairly narrow. It is great if your target audience is composed of young male high earners but less helpful at present if your product is aimed at elderly women.

This factor reduces the projectability of data recorded over the Internet - if the sample is too narrow it is difficult to use the reactions of this sample to project the reactions of the total market segment.

Using the Internet to collect primary data

Form surveys on the Web

Form surveys on the Web are perhaps the most widely used market research tool on the Internet. Interactive forms enable users to interact with your Web pages.

You can use interactive forms built into Web pages to:

O **ask questions about your Web site**
O **solicit information from users concerning your products or services**
O **find out more about your users**

Forms soliciting user information can be installed as a prerequisite for accessing your site.

*An example is **The Electronic Telegraph** Web site <http://www. telegraph.co.uk/>. To maintain the Electronic Telegraph as a free service, they need to attract advertisers and therefore have to collate demographics on users. Registration allows them to compile accurate data about the number of people reading The Electronic Telegraph each day, and what stories and sections they find most useful.*

Worryingly, the Sixth WWW User Survey (December 1996) conducted by the **Graphics, Visualisation and Usability Centre** <http://www. cc.gatech.edu/gvu/user_surveys/> revealed that 33.5% of respondents said they falsified information they provided when registering to use a Web site. Therefore information collected in this way must be carefully interpreted.

Making your form short and speedy to complete, or reducing the number of obligatory fields to complete, may also reduce the number of users who write almost anything down just to get to your site. Offering a reward, such as access to valuable information, may also encourage people to supply correct details. A fully functional Internet survey based around traditional research methodologies may be more appropriate to collect serious data.

Sampling

The least expensive means of recruiting for Internet research is through uninvited, 'drop-in', visitors to the Web site. This is not the most reliable or accurate way of obtaining a sample because it depends on how much traffic is generated to the site and the positioning of the survey in that site. Respondents obtained this way may not reflect your organisation's target market and you may not get enough in a specified time-frame to be of use. One way of getting around the problem of non-representative samples is to use only those completed surveys that match a set of pre-determined criteria corresponding to the target market, such as males between 30-40 in full employment.

Self-selection

One worry when conducting market research over the Internet is that it is self-selecting, leading to misleading results if respondents are significantly different from the population sample. This problem can be addressed by conducting 'invitation only' surveys and screening before allowing potential respondents to participate. Potential participants are invited to complete a screening questionnaire asking for details such as demographics or, perhaps, products or services used. Then, if the answers to these questions fit the criteria for the survey, the respondent is invited back to participate in the full survey.

Response rate

Response rates can be low on the Internet because respondents have to pay - telephone charges and in some cases on-line charges - for the privilege of completing your survey. Response rates can be increased by the use of incentives such as cash, prizes or even a promise to send the results of the survey. Often the incentive is access to free information or entertainment on the site itself and the small price to pay for this offer is a few user details.

German magazine **Stern** *<http://www.stern.de/tv/> employs a useful service to invite you to supply information. You enter the details of your favourite actor and when that actor appears on TV you are notified by e-mail. As you become more involved in the site you are encouraged to submit further information about your TV viewing habits. This information is then used to attract advertisers.*

A flexible medium

An interactive survey on the World Wide Web can be done by simply taking a traditional text-based survey questionnaire and placing it as it stands on your Web site.

31

However, the flexibility of the medium means that you can experiment with ways of presenting surveys in a more inviting and less obtrusive way. The key is to get people to submit useful information without even realising it. For instance, you could pepper your Web site with short questions that can be responded to quickly.

You could also think about running your survey over several pages, making it a little more interactive and manageable.

The Web also has a multimedia capability. This means that you can use audiovisuals and record reactions to such material, much as you might via personal interview surveys.

Guidelines for designing your on-line survey:

○ All the question types commonly found in traditional market research can be implemented on the Internet, including open-ended questions, dichotomous questions and multiple-choice questions

○ Your survey should be short and easy to respond to

○ Use pick lists with several options to choose from including a default option (eg. a list of countries with UK as the default option) and radio buttons where users click on a button to indicate a preference or response to an answer - these are easier and quicker to use than having to ask respondents to type things out and you are likely to get more answers

○ If you include compulsory questions - that is, questions that must be completed before the respondent can submit the survey - let them know this is the case, pointing out which questions are compulsory, perhaps by using different colours for optional and compulsory questions

○ Assure respondents that private information will remain confidential

○ Ask for an e-mail address - people are more likely to be truthful once they have identified themselves and you can weed out multiple entries

○ Respondents will appreciate some kind of response from you, even if this is an automated e-mail response thanking them for participating in the survey

○ **Let respondents know what the data is going to be used for, and the benefits to them and your organisation of having them complete the survey**
○ **Always include a tick box that gives users the option not to allow information to be used for direct mail shots**

A number of companies offer software to assist you in compiling your on-line surveys.

Decision Architects <*http://www.decisionarc.com/*> *provide software called MarketSight which contains a library of questions that can easily be altered, wizards that lead users step-by-step through the questionnaire design process, and simple analytical tools such as cross-tabulations and frequencies. Also, it provides the option of creating an HTML-coded document for use as a survey tool on a Web site.*

DataStar Inc <*http://www.surveystar.com/*> *is a US company specialising in survey management and data processing. They offer help with questionnaire design and electronic surveys.*

On-line panel research

Another form of on-line survey is the on-line panel. Panels consist of a sample of respondents who have agreed to complete surveys at requested intervals over time. They are notified by e-mail that they have surveys waiting, and then visit the research company's Web site to complete the questionnaires.

The advantage of on-line panels is that they can be used to record changes in consumer attitudes or behaviour and are useful in evaluating products or services over a set period of time. However, they can introduce sample-composition bias. Careful screening and by-invitation-only panels can reduce this.

There are companies that specialise in conducting on-line panels for clients.

E-valuations Research <*http://www.e-valuations.com/company.htm*> *has a research site called Questions.net which assembles a group of willing research participants by offering them incentives to answer survey questions.*

They are invited to visit the client's site to answer the questions provided. Clients can pick the target group that is best-suited to providing the specific information they need.

*The **NPD On-line Panel** <http://www.npd.com> can carry out research on advert awareness, attitude and usage, concept testing, focus groups, longitudinal tracking, product testing, segmentation and more via its on-line panel.*

On-line focus groups

On-line focus groups are also currently being used for market research. These are typically conducted in chat rooms with a moderator to prompt questions and stimulate dialogue on a particular product or organisation.

A chat room is a special area on a Web site - entered using a password - where users meet at a specified time and participate in a discussion by typing their contributions on their keyboard, which are then displayed in seconds on the Web page for the whole group to see and respond to.

Cyber Dialogue <http://www.cyberdialogue.com/> run on-line focus groups with moderators.

On-line focus groups have the advantage over traditional focus groups in that they are much cheaper to carry out. Organisations can also conduct them in overseas markets at no extra cost. Unlike their traditional counterparts, on-line focus groups cannot be used to gather data through observation - although this may change with improvements in video conferencing facilities over the Web.

***Greenfield On-line** <http://www.greenfieldgroup.com/> is a company which conducts Internet surveys and questionnaires on a wide range of topics.*

Their Public Surveys are open to anyone who completes their Sign-Up Survey. Many of the surveys carry an incentive such as prizes and money. They also have Invitation Only Surveys which are sponsored by their clients. Respondents must meet the screening criteria for that study. This often involves their demographics and/or the types of products and services they use. If respondents qualify, they go through a brief screening survey and are then invited to participate. The survey name, the user name and the survey password, are then e-mailed so that they can take part. After having participated, respondents are eligible for an incentive compensation.

The company is quite clear that information provided is completely confidential and is used to help companies develop products and services.

Greenfield On-line also conducts on-line focus groups where four to six people are invited to join Greenfield's 'moderators' at a specified time in one of their chat rooms. Participants spend an hour or so discussing a topic or a series of related topics. Participants in on-line focus groups receive an incentive for their effort - often cash or other valuable prizes.

Cookies

Cookies are small data files used by Web sites to store information about a user. They have the advantage of requiring no direct input from the user. They are used to gather information about users' behaviour and preferences in Web sites.

When a user visits a Web site a cookie can be sent from that site to the user's Web Browser and then stored on their hard disk. The cookie can record the user's movements within that site and other information about them such as their e-mail address.

Each time a user visits a Web site the Browser looks on the user's hard disk to see whether a cookie exists for that site, if one does it is sent to the server as part of the request for the Web page, the server can then interpret the information held in the cookie and return appropriate content.

They are increasingly being used to monitor the movements of individuals within Web sites for market research and linked to marketing databases which control banner adverts for targeted advertising.

Cookies are a valuable market research tool because they can tell companies how individuals spend their time on the Internet. They can also keep track of an individual's interests by recording the search words that they enter into search engines. This is done with the user's consent and so cookies are not 100% reliable for market research or targeted advertising because users can always delete cookie files or set their Browsers to notify them of cookie files and refuse to accept them.

Market research via e-mail

Market research conducted by e-mail must be approached with care and a full understanding of the rules of netiquette that regulate the posting of unsolicited e-mail on the Internet. Unsolicited e-mail is not welcomed on the Internet and may result in negative feelings towards your organisation and a reluctance on behalf of people to co-operate in your market research activities on- or off-line.

E-mail response built into your Web pages provides guaranteed user names and e-mail addresses as this information is automatically included in the mail header attached to the e-mail.

Decisive Technology <*http://www.worklife.com/decisive.htm*> *offers a comprehensive software package called Decisive Survey which is used for designing and executing e-mail surveys.*

This software can set up an anonymous response facility, automatically track response status and conduct follow-up management, to consolidate data automatically, to export it, or to conduct statistical analyses.

Market research via USENET Newsgroups

USENET is a worldwide network of discussion groups on thousands of subjects ranging from special interests to professional practice. There are over 16,000 of them, called Newsgroups. You can request or provide information in Newsgroups or start a new discussion simply by posting messages to the Newsgroup. In marketing terms, Newsgroups are an excellent people resource with the added advantage that users declare their interests by the mere fact that they have subscribed to a Newsgroup on a particular topic.

Posting surveys indiscriminately to Newsgroups is not recommended and postings of a commercial nature are often frowned upon. There are, however, some discrete and effective ways of capitalising on these people resources for marketing purposes without causing offence among the Internet community.

For example you can:

○ **post strategic queries to a few relevant discussion groups. Eg, if you come across a mention of your product, service or company in a Newsgroup (DejaNews <http://www. dejanews. com/> is a search engine which will tell you which Newsgroups your product, service or company has been mentioned in) you could post a relevant question to the group**

○ **Many Newsgroups discuss particular products and services that are related to the subject and it is worth observing these discussions and posting relevant contributions with a pointer to a survey at your Web site and an invitation to people to voice their opinions and reactions**

Mailing lists

Mailing Lists can also be used to build up user profiles. A real mine of information, mailing lists are similar to USENET Newsgroups in that they provide a forum for discussion.

They are different from Newsgroups because messages come directly to you in the form of e-mail. Mailing list discussions are conducted entirely by e-mail.

By posting an e-mail to a central e-mail account known as a Listserver your message is automatically forwarded to all subscribers to that mailing list.

Like Newsgroups, mailing lists exist on all sorts of topics. In fact, many Newsgroups have an associated mailing list.

When a user sends an e-mail request for information to a Listserver the Listserver responds by e-mail. The user's e-mail request to the Listserver can reveal not only the user's location and e-mail address but also their interests - based on which particular category of information the user requested from the Listserver.

Logfiles

Logfiles sit on your Web server and record who is visiting your site, how they arrived there, which country they are from, how long they stay, which is the most popular content accessed and when.

There are limitations with the application of logfiles to accurate compilation of meaningful user statistics. These are fully discussed in Chapter 10.

Using the Internet to collect secondary data

The Internet is a vast repository of research, ranging from reports to databases. Most of it can be found on the Web. For example, there are many surveys on Internet demographics available on the Web itself. See Chapter 2 for further details on demographic surveys to be found on the Internet. At <http://www.Webworldinc.com/div/ocb1127B.htm> you can find links to a number of free market research reports.

Finding Information on the Internet

Finding information on the Web can be like looking for a needle in a haystack. Luckily, there are tools to make your research easier.

Search engines

Search engines are accessed like any other Web page by typing an address into your Web Browser. A Web page will then appear with a window box for you to type in a keyword, or words. The search engine will then go off and search for Web pages (and/or Newsgroups) that match your key words and return the results as a list of links to those pages.

Some of the most popular search engines include:

○ **Alta Vista** *< http://www.altavista.digital.com/ >* **Lists 16 million pages and enables precise searches including searches for phrases.**

- Yell <http://www.yell.co.uk/> A UK search engine listing UK Web sites.
- Lycos *<http://www.lycos.com/>* A general search engine.
- YAHOO *<http://www.yahoo.com/>* A directory of sites selected and reviewed by the compilers.
- Excite <http://www.excite.com/> Allows you to search for phrases.

All search engines are different and vary in their scope and speed. It is best to use more than one. Some will search Newsgroups as well as the Web. For example, **DejaNews** http://www.dejanews.com/ and **InfoSeek** http://www.infoseek.com

They also include various options to refine your search, including searching by phrase, natural language searches or the use of Boolean operators such as AND, OR and NOT.

On-line subscription services

These services, dubbed the Outernet, offer market research information for a fee. They can be accessed via the Internet using a password. More powerful than information available on the Web, they allow searches for market information and new trends as well as searches across multiple databases.

DataStar *<http://www.rs.ch/krinfo/products/dsweb/index.htm>* *contains 700 business databases. The service costs 80 Swiss francs a year, plus charges for databases searched and items downloaded.*

Push

Push, or Web broadcasting as it is also known, enables users to have information which matches a predefined set of criteria delivered to their desktops directly without having to go out and seek it.

Software such as PointCast and Castanet delivers information to the desktop via a screensaver or scrolling window. New market research reports can be delivered to you as they come out. See Chapter 9 for more information on Push.

Intelligent Agents

An Intelligent Agent is a piece of software that you can 'train' or give a set of instructions to, such as finding information on a certain topic for you on the Web, and it will go away and do it.

Some are autonomous - that is, they carry on searching for you even after your computer is switched off. They place themselves on a Server and report back when they have found something.

Intelligent agents can be personalised or trained to adapt to their users likes and dislikes, tastes and preferences. They are also flexible in that they have initiative and can offer suggestions.

Autonomy *<http://www.agentware.com> has a number of personalised intelligent agents. For example Web Researcher enables you to research topics on the Internet more effectively. Take any agent you have trained about a subject, drag it to the Web Researcher and your agent is released onto the Web to find relevant material and bring it back to you.*

Your agent can learn from experience and become more efficient at searching. You can 'talk' to your agent (which is represented by a dog) in plain English. And train it by dragging and dropping it onto a training button. In the future, your agent will be able to go to a kennel located on Servers and carry out searches on your behalf while you are disconnected. Agents will also be able to interact with each other and swap information on similar searches.

Validity of information obtained on the Internet

The validity of information sourced on the Web should be carefully scrutinised as these days it is so easy and cheap to publish information on the Web that anyone can do it. This means that as well as a lot of valuable and reliable information out there, there is an equal amount of unreliable or false information. So how do you sort the wheat from the chaff?

When using information sourced on the Web bear in mind that it may not always be entirely accurate. Information does not go through as rigorous a checking procedure as it might through traditional means. For example, scientific papers may not have been through the usual peer reviewing system that they have in real life. It is always a good idea to do a few spot checks of information found on the Internet - a quick phone call may be sufficient.

It is also difficult to judge the authenticity of a document or site on the Web. What may appear to be an informative site offering advice on health, may in fact turn out to be written by a pharmaceutical company. Look out for more 'official' sites and sites that have established off-line equivalents, such as The Electronic Telegraph.

Information on the Web may also be out of date. Look out for dates on Web sites to make sure that information really is the most recent available.

Some useful marketing Web sites

The following sites contain useful links to marketing reports, surveys and other marketing resources which may help you with your market research.

- **Researchit** < http://www.iTools.com/research-it/ >
- **Marketing Research Index** < http://www.reinartz.com/ >
- **Adweek** < http://www.adweek.com/ >
- **Tenagra Corporation** < http://marketing.tenagra.com/imr.html
- **Marketing Week** < http://www.marketing-week.co.uk/mw0001/ >
- **The Chartered Institute of Marketing** < http://www.cim.co.uk/ >
- **Wilson Web Marketing Info Centre ™** < http://www.wilsonweb.com/webmarket/ >
- **Interactive Media in Retail Group** < http://www.imrg.co.uk >
- **Gartner** < http://www.gartner.com >
- **Jupiter Communications** < http://www.jup.com/ >
- **CyberAtlas** < http://www.cyberatlas.com/ >

Summary

- **The Internet can be used to collect both primary and secondary data.**

- Interactive forms on the Web are a very useful way of collecting information.
- To get around the problem of self-selection on the Internet it is worth considering invitation-only or screening.
- Incentives such as cash, prizes or access to free valuable information can help to increase the response rate of your survey.
- Panels and focus groups - two traditional market research methods - are possible on the Web.
- A new way of gathering information on your target market is with Cookies - small data files that are downloaded with a Web site and sit on users' computers collecting information about them.
- Market research via e-mail should be approached carefully and within the norms of netiquette - the informal rules governing behaviour on the Internet.
- There is an abundance of information such as marketing reports, research and business databases available on the Internet. However, it is not always easy to find and may not always be reliable.
- New technologies such as Push and Intelligent Agents are making the job of finding information on the Internet much easier.

5 Advertising on the Internet

Advertising on the Internet has a relatively short track record and as such has had little time to prove itself. The number of direct sales attributable to Internet advertising is still low and on-line ads have yet to prove that they can achieve returns on investments equal to those of other media.

However, advertisers often misunderstand the medium and its properties and are consequently trying to fit a square peg into a round hole. Many Internet advertising campaigns imitate traditional methods. It should be remembered that Web users are seeking information as well as entertainment. Advertisers must address these needs in their on-line campaigns in order to communicate their message effectively.

Most advertising on the Internet is done via the World Wide Web. The Web is an exciting medium for advertising as it can display text, graphics, sound and video. Web adverts grab attention and act as a point of information, point of sampling (ie. in the case of software) and, if required, a point of sale.

Internet advertising includes Web banners, buttons, links, site-sponsorship deals, as well as entire Web sites created simply as an advertising venue.

Responsible low-level Internet advertising has become a more tolerated part of the Web, as users accept that advertising revenue makes it possible for Web publishers to offer content without charge. It is up to advertisers and content publishers not to abuse this acceptance by swamping the Web with advertising and adversely affecting the user's experience - the result of which could be lost future Web users or an increase in advert filtering software.

Advertising on the Internet is unregulated but voluntary organisations such as the Internet Advertising Bureau <http://www.edelman.com/IAB/index.html> make recommendations to advertisers and publishers.

Why advertise on the Internet?

○ Your competitors may already be ahead of the game and using the Internet to advertise their products and services. By being left behind you may be sending the wrong signals to your consumers about your ability to maintain a competitive edge and adopt new marketing media channels.

○ To reach new audiences. The Internet is gaining in popularity in the entertainment and information stakes and winning consumers away from traditional media such as magazines and TV. Therefore, by advertising on the Internet you can reach an audience that is not watching TV or reading magazines. Bear in mind, however, that the Internet is still not a mass marketing medium.

○ Advertising on the Internet is an inexpensive method of advertising compared with traditional print and broadcast options.

○ Advertising on the Internet is measurable. It is easy to monitor the number of hits an advertisement receives. You can determine how well your advert is doing on a weekly basis, including how many people have visited, which parts they stayed in for the longest period and how much time they spent there. There are, however, factors to take into account when interpreting the number of hits an advert receives. See Chapter 10 for further details.

○ On-line advertising creates the opportunity for immediate interaction with, and feedback from, consumers while traditional media do not. Interactive advertising closes the gap between producer contact and consumer response since feedback and response from consumers is quasi-instantaneous. There is huge potential for the Web both to build customer relationships and evaluate the effectiveness of an advertising campaign at the same time. For example, on the Internet an advertiser can give a potential customer an interactive product demonstration and comparison. The customer can instantly request additional information or even make a purchase on the spot. That is impossible using traditional advertising vehicles. The consumer is in control - on-line advertising empowers the consumer in ways that traditional media never could. If your advertising campaign offers the consumer a chance to exercise that power through interactivity, you are more likely to be successful.

O   You can implement an Internet advertising campaign in much less time than would be required through traditional media.

O   The Web's forte lies in its ability to provide extensive product information unlike traditional advertising media which are not suitable for carrying large amounts of product information. Think how little you can say about a product on an advertising billboard. On a Web site you can offer all the information you like and then leave it to the reader to decide what information he or she wants to see about products or services.

O   It is possible to deliver marketing messages over the Web to a very narrowly defined target group. For example, if someone looks for health related sites, you can be fairly confident that they are interested in health issues. You can then programme the site so that they receive health related adverts.

O   Your Internet advertisement is not necessarily time-based. In the case of a Web site, it can be accessed 24 hours a day. In addition, adverts are not time-limited, storing material on the Web is very cheap compared to archiving information via traditional methods. This means that your advertising can be permanently available. On the Levi <http://www.levi.com> site, for example, you can find their archive material on many of their advertising campaigns.

O   The Internet is suitable for advertising products and
     services to both local and global audiences.

However, there are some negative issues that advertisers must bear in mind:

O   The medium is entirely self selecting. It is unlike other forms
     of advertising in that users must seek out the advertising
     rather than have the advertising brought to them as it is on
     TV. So there must be a reason for people to visit.

O   Web advertising does not sell itself. Once a brand site
     exists, it must then be promoted. Think about dedicating
     at least 20% of your interactive advertising budget to
     promoting your site both on and off-line. (See Chapter 7
     for further details on marketing your site.)

O   On-line adverts must be appealing to users and make them
     want to return by providing value-added content. It no
     longer suffices to have a highly creative advert featuring all
     the latest technology - this will not be enough to make
     users come back. Advertising on the Internet must be
     content-driven. It must be informative, entertaining and
     functional and above all it must change.

*Levi <http://www.levi.com> is an advertising site created by UK and US Web
specialists and advertising agencies to provide a content driven on-line
lifestyle magazine which appeals to the youth market. It also uses creativity
which is appropriate for a fashion brand.*

O   Measuring the success of your on-line advertising
     campaign is not straightforward. You may be able to
     measure the number of visitors to your Web site and the
     way they browsed the site, but their response will be a mix
     of on-line and off-line reactions which is less quantifiable.

O   When developing a media plan, advertisers should always
     consider whether the content of the message is appropriate
     for the Internet. For example, food may look very appealing
     in a full-colour, glossy magazine, but less so when seen on a

46

screen-based low resolution medium such as the Internet. However, the Internet is a very good medium for showing off certain product features by using multimedia presentations with sound and video.

Banner advertising

Banner adverts are the most popular advertising method on the Internet. Banner advertisements are single 480x60 pixel graphics, either animated or static, that appear on Web pages.

The graphic usually links the user to the advertising company's Web site when clicked on. They are typically rotated - one appearing over another over a period of time - on the page.

Banner ads currently account for approximately 80 per cent of all Internet advertisements.

Programmes such as SelectCast <http://www.aptex.com/select.htm> can be added to an advertiser's Web site to observe which pages users request. The software develops profiles for all site visitors, analyses and groups profiles to identify users with similar interests, and then delivers designated adverts to selected groups as they move through the site.

This is used in search engine Web sites, where a user types in 'recipes' for example and a banner for a restaurant may appear above their search results.

Creating an effective banner advert

Typically, you only have a couple of seconds to make an impact with a banner advert. The purpose of a banner advert is to get people to click on it and go direct to your site. Focus should therefore be on achieving this rather than creativity. Positioning and content are also key factors in creating an effective banner advert.

O   **The best place to put your banner advert is at the top of a page.**

○ Animation related to the message has been proven to raise response rate. Flat, billboard-type adverts are less effective.

○ The more interactivity and involvement that is created by banners, the higher the click-through rates. For example, many banners use forms linked to search engines which allow users to go straight to the information they want. Conde Net <http://www.condenet.com/> ran a banner advert for Epicurious where you could search the recipe and database directly and then go straight to the relevant section on the site. The food banner generated a click-through of 52%.

○ More complex adverts using Java and Shockwave cannot be viewed by all users - they may not have the latest plug-ins or available bandwidth. You should think about communicating with the lowest common denominator.

○ Ensure your adverts don't annoy users by taking a long time to download. Internet Fast Forward <http://www.privnet.com> is a software programme that allows users to fast-forward through bandwidth-hungry advertisements. Don't give your audience a reason to use it.

○ Using the words 'click here' on your banner is an effective way to get people to act.

○ The most effective banner adverts are those that refer to a specific brand, product or service rather than a company logo - people are more likely to want to find out about a product than a company.

○ Adverts expire. Once a person sees a banner twice, there is no point in showing it again and response rates have been shown to diminish after two views. To be effective, advertisers must rotate ads.

○ The advertiser's site must not disappoint and as much attention should go into it as for your banner advert. The

Web site is the ultimate goal, the banner is simply a hook to entice users to the Web site which is the ultimate advert.

Web sites

An increasing amount of advertising is done via Web sites dedicated to promoting brands, products or services. Advertising agencies are working with Web producers to create advertorials with strong branding and related content.

Ben & Jerry's <*http://www.benjerry.com/index.html*> *site is fun and entertaining and it is an effective extension of the brand.*

Absolut Vodka <*http://www.absolutvodka.com/*>. *The site is captivating with features such as a 'Bot bar and Human Ant Farm. Interestingly, the corporate logo is not featured once.*

Networks

Networks are becoming an increasingly popular way of both delivering content and as a vehicle for advertising. Networks are large groups of sites, generally grouped by theme of content but also by geographical location.

They are a blessing for advertisers as they group together content that is otherwise dispersed over the Web. Networks offer a more focused way of targeting content and traffic.

They can offer greater advantages to advertisers than single content sites, eg.

O   **large audiences**
O   **better demographics, site statistics and therefore targeting. Economies of scale will dictate that networks will be able to provide better tracking and management facilities**
O   **legitimacy. Networks vet sites - therefore provide greater assurance of the ability to deliver traffic and appropriate content**

Types of network

- One type of network offers advertisers a selection from hundreds or thousands of sites of varying content. One such network is DoubleClick <http://www.doubleclick.net>.

- Other networks are appearing that are geographically bound, catering for local and regional markets.

- Webcast networks such as PointCast can deliver advertising to the desktop in response to customers' needs.

- Content based networks offer context-sensitive advertising where content is linked thematically to advertising.

- Directory services such as Yahoo!, yet another type of network, offer mass traffic.

These networks benefit from having better access to advertisers through their sales force, financial stability amidst new emerging pricing structures for advertising on the Internet, the ability to invest in the technologies needed to deliver advertising-supported content and the flexibility to try out new and innovative content.

Sponsorship

Sponsorship means that a client will agree to finance a section of a Web site, or even an entire service.

A more cost-effective example of the technique was used by Condé Nast <http://www.condenast.co.uk> with their long-running Champagne Mercier promotion. The Mercier site is hosted on the Condé Nast Web site and is specifically plugged in the Tatler Guide to Restaurants presented by Champagne Mercier. You can browse through the restaurant site, which has links to Mercier and offers you the chance to win in two Mercier competitions.

Links

Links from on-line directories and search engines and from other people's Web sites are a form of advertising and are free.

Interstitials

Interstitials are 5 to 10 second animated ads which appear without having to click on anything. They take up the whole of the screen and are played before receiving the content of the Web site they are hosted on. They can be used to deliver higher quality animated adverts with a large amount of information. They offer a more creative and intrusive way of delivering an advertising message. However, they can also annoy Web users who are looking for information and have to endure 10 seconds of unsolicited advertising before reaching it. Users have no control over the advert, many do not link to the advertiser's site and are not interactive. It is also difficult to take down details as they run fairly quickly.

Interstitials are very new and have not developed to their full potential. Until now, they have been mainly found on push services such as PointCast, but are becoming more common on Web sites.

If you do plan to use interstitials keep them short, small and easy to download and make it clear that it is an advertisement so that people don't think they have gone to the wrong site. Do not repeat the advert every time the user goes to your home page.

Jupiter Communications <http://www.jup.com> predicts that on-line advertisers will increasingly turn from banners to sponsorships and interstitials and that by the year 2001 advertisers will dedicate, on average, one-quarter of their budgets to sponsorships and interstitials, with the remaining half going to banners.

Video, audio, chat and enhanced interactivity are new features that are starting to appear in the latest on-line advertisements.

Berkeley Systems' *<http://www.bezerk.com> on-line entertainment network beZerk delivers interstitial ads, TV-style, during breaks in their on-line pop-culture quiz 'You Don't Know Jack - the Netshow'. During a 25 minute* *programme there are three interstitial breaks. These are full-screen animations, with soundtracks lasting 10 seconds. It costs $140 for each 1000 viewings of a 10-second interstitial.*

Placing adverts

Once you have decided what type of advertising is appropriate, the next step is to place your advert. It is advantageous to place your banner advert on a site that has a guaranteed minimum 10, 000 visitors a day and that is likely to be used by your target market, for example, one of the popular search engines. These do, however, charge a high premium for the privilege of placing a banner advert on their site. Banner adverts on popular sites such as Netscape or Lycos can go for $20, 000 a month.

Search engines

At least half the advertising on the World Wide Web is done via search engines. Their attraction is their ability to target people according to what they are looking for. Further enhancement comes from the growth of targeted search engines such as regional ones and those aimed at young people. The problem with placing banner ads in search engines is that people normally use the search engine for a specific purpose - to get somewhere. They are often not ready to go somewhere else by following through a banner advert to an advertiser's site.

Your advert is linked to a set of key words, so, if someone makes a search using the key word 'wine' and this is one of your key words then your advert will be displayed. Key words should include company name, product or service name and generic terms associated with it. It is worth paying extra for exclusivity of a key word - otherwise your advert will be rotated amongst many others, perhaps even some from your competitors.

Impressions

Typically a media buyer will book a number (usually in the tens of thousands) of impressions (an impression, also known as an eyeball, is the number of times a visitor views your advert on a requested page) - a single impression costs around 3 pence. You may or may not have a time limit imposed to use up your impressions.

Impressions can now also be linked to the searcher's domain names. So, for example, if anyone from a specific domain such as .co.uk domain uses a search engine they will get to see your advert.

Content-driven sites

Targeted sites are becoming more popular for advert placement, ie. those sites that have specific content aimed at a narrowly defined audience, eg. magazine publishers Emap Internet Sales <http://www.internet-sales.com>, Playboy magazine <http://www.playboy.com>, HotWired <http://www.hotwired.com> and Times Warner Pathfinder <http://pathfinder.com/ >.

They can offer appropriate content, enabling advertisers to place adverts on Web sites they know match the profile of their prospective market, and higher click-through rates. The information available from the Times Warner Pathfinder site is an education for all would-be Internet marketers.

Time Warner Pathfinder <http://pathfinder.com/> The Time Warner site contains content from its magazine, television, music and film divisions, as well as information from selected outside providers. These include TIME, Life, People, Fortune, Entertainment Weekly, Atlantic Records, Warner Bros. Records, Warner Bros. Animation, DC Comics and more. The site receives more than 10 million pageviews per week (83% male, 17% female). It offers a standard advertising package with a combination of banners and buttons - advertising 'Gateways' - hot-linked directly to advertisers' Web sites. These Gateways are rotated through Pathfinder's high-traffic areas and/or selected areas of interest, so adverts get maximum visibility and targeting.

Pathfinder is one of the largest and highest-trafficked content-based sites on the Web. Advertising on the site will reach a large, highly educated, upscale audience that is growing rapidly every day and supported by an ongoing print and television advertising campaign in Time Inc. magazines and on Time Warner cable systems. Pathfinder also provides advertisers with weekly reports on the progress of their campaign. Their marketing department regularly assists leading advertisers in creating on-line content and customised advertising applications.

The demographic breakdown of the site audience according to the Pathfinder Interactive Advertising Survey, April 1996 suggests an average user to be 38yrs old, to have attended graduate college or more, and with an average disposable income of $70, 000.

37% of all users are on Pathfinder 1+ hours a week
55% of all users click on Pathfinder's ads 1+ times per hour while at home, 37% while at work
57% of all Pathfinder users always/sometimes bookmark advertisers' Web sites
49% of all Pathfinder users click beyond an advertiser's home page
49% of all Pathfinder users stated advertisements on the Web are effective in introducing them to new companies/products

Pathfinder users feel advertisements on the Internet are more effective than in other media:

because they are non intrusive (76%)
because they are accessible 24 hours a day (61%)
because they are more informative (48%)

The Pathfinder site offers to help advertisers create a unique and exclusive on-line advertising and marketing environment through a blend of on-line advertorial, contests, sweepstakes, interactive games, database generation and other specialised advertising applications.

Paying for your advertising

Buying space for banner adverts is not an exact science and very much in the experimental stages - most media buyers go for sites listed in top site listings directories such as PC Meter.

It is not uncommon to use a Web broker to negotiate advertising space as they have more experience, they often represent several hundred Web sites and can offer demographic and measurement information. Webconnect <http://www.webconnect.net/> is one of the best known media placements for services for the Internet. WebConnect can also create networks of Web sites specifically designed to meet clients' needs and provide tracking and reporting services to see how well an advert is doing.

Some Web sites such as HotWired <http://www.hotwired.com> keep some of their advertising windows for good causes, either free or at a reduced rate.

Cost per thousand impressions (CPM)

Currently adverts are paid for per thousand impressions (CPM). For popular search engines such as Yahoo! and Excite this costs in the region of £30 per thousand impressions. A banner on a search engine home page costs about £4000 week.

Click-through

CPM is not a satisfactory pricing model, translated as it has been from traditional media. A more appropriate method would be per 'click through' - the number of people who click on a banner advert and get to the advertiser's Web site. Banner advertising click through rates are still relatively low at 5%. Paying for click through is more expensive than impressions.

A new initiative by advertising network DoubleClick Inc <http://www.doubleclick.net/> called DoubleClick Direct charges advertisers only when users act, as for instance by completing a questionnaire or buying a product.

Banner advert exchange services

If you want the benefits of banner advertising without paying the high premiums associated with them you could always try a banner advert exchange service. You agree to host banner adverts supplied by the exchange service on your site. In return, you add your own advert to the distribution list and choose which types of site you want to appear on. The more clicks that the adverts on your site get, then the more times your advert is shown on other sites. Information on the number of times your advert has been clicked on, and how many times your advert has appeared, is provided by the service.

Link Exchange <http://www.linkexchange.com/> is one of the most popular exchange services with 100, 000 sites on its books.

Swapping banners

One way of getting free banner advertising is to swap banners with another site. Find a site that you think could generate relevant traffic to your site and offer to carry their advert in exchange for yours.

Classified advertising

Classified advertising also has a place on the Internet with many local and national classified advertising sites, advertising anything from boats to personal ads. LOOT the popular UK free classified advertising newspaper, for instance, has a site at <http://www.loot.com> which contains about 70,000 classified ads a day.

The advantage of classifieds on-line is the ability to search for something specific using keywords and a search engine, rather than to have to wade through acres of small print.

Advertising in Newsgroups

In general, advertising is not permitted in Newsgroups. Read the Frequently Asked Questions (FAQ) for your chosen Newsgroup carefully - this should tell you what advertising practices are considered to be acceptable within that Newsgroup.

See Chapter 8 for further information on marketing via Newsgroups.

Advertising via e-mail

More people have e-mail access than Web access. Used appropriately, e-mail can be used effectively for advertising your product or service.

E-mail is becoming more and more sophisticated with features such as embedding live links to Web sites in your e-mail. You can also add file attachments to your e-mail.

However, beware when advertising your site via e-mail. The practice of spamming or mass e-mailing to a 'cold' audience is considered bad Netiquette amongst the Internet community and will result in your Internet access being pulled. Recipients have to pay to receive your unsolicited e-mail.

The Sixth WWW User Survey (December 1996) conducted by the Graphics, Visualisation and Usability Centre <http://www.cc.gatech.edu/gvu/user_surveys/> revealed that 46% of respondents said they deleted unwanted e-mail, while only 9% actually read it.

An effective way of using e-mail to advertise your products or services is to use mailing lists compiled from your Web site of people who have indicated a willingness to receive information by e-mail from your organisation.

Netiquette

Acceptable advertising practices on the Internet are governed by the informal guidelines to behaviour on the Internet referred to as 'netiquette'. A blacklist of Internet advertisers <http://math-www.uni-paderborn.de/~axel/BL/blacklist.html> has been set up to highlight inappropriate advertising in Newsgroups and via junk e-mail.

Generating revenue through advertising

Many content providers are pursuing advertising revenue to finance their operations. Some sites are actually making a profit based solely on advertising revenue. But bear in mind that the on-line advertising spend of those companies with the largest advertising budgets is currently less than 2 percent and that the Internet is still not a mass marketing medium.

You will be more successful in raising advertising revenue if:

O **your site is content-driven and highly targeted**
O **you are able to provide demographic details of users and to target advertising according to demographics, interests and domain.**

You will need to purchase advertisement rotation and tracking software if you want to display adverts on your site.

Combining traditional advertising with Internet advertising

On-line advertising should only be part of your advertising programme. An effective advertising strategy will integrate media to communicate a message and reach an appropriate audience. You must ask yourself the same questions as for other media when determining whether the Internet is a viable medium.

Referencing your Internet adverts from your traditional adverts gives your audience another way of accessing information about your organisation and its products or services, therefore helping build awareness. It also begins to address the low content problem of the traditional media. Many advertisements these days have a Web site URL posted on them. Bear in mind that users do not want to see an exact copy of your traditional communication on the Web.

Guinness <http://www.guinness.com/> have very effectively integrated their TV advertising campaigns with their Web advertising campaigns. The Guinness screensaver - an animated clip themed on the Guinness adverts - was hugely popular, appearing on many PC users' desktops.

Summary

O   Internet advertising includes banner adverts, interstitials, links and site sponsorship.

O   Internet advertising addresses the low content problem of traditional advertising media, enabling advertisers to provide more information about their products or services.

O   Networks of sites are a good channel for advertising as they provide a more focused way of targeting content and traffic.

O   Interstitials - TV-like, full-screen animated adverts - and site sponsorship are set to become the Internet advertising channels of the future, along with banner adverts.

- ○ Search engines and targeted content-driven sites are the best for placing your adverts.
- ○ Advertisers typically pay for advertising by the number of times users see their advert. This is being replaced by paying for advertising according to the number of people who click on an advert.
- ○ Free advertising can be obtained by swapping adverts or reciprocal links.
- ○ Mass, unsolicited advertising via e-mail and Newsgroups is not well received on the Internet. You must abide by the informal rules of netiquette if you wish to use e-mail and Newsgroups for advertising.
- ○ The most effective advertising campaign is one which integrates different media to communicate your marketing message.

6 Selling over the Internet

A survey carried out by Harris Research for KPMG Management Consulting <http://www.kpmg.co.uk> (*Electronic Commerce Research* report, KPMG, London 0171-311 8786) on electronic commerce reveals that the UK's top companies expect almost one in five of their sales to come directly via the Internet in five year's time, representing a total of about £170 billion in income. Direct sales attributed to the Net are predicted to grow from two to three per cent today to about 17 per cent over the next five years. The Internet as marketplace is certainly on the way to becoming commercially viable and acceptable to consumers. The report reveals that large UK companies expect the Internet to have a considerable impact on their business. The expectation is that the Internet will be used heavily for electronic commerce by 2000.

The Internet can be used to complete all activities in the traditional sales cycle, from providing information about products and services and your organisation, through purchase, ordering and payment, to distribution of certain products, and customer support.

The Internet can be used both for business-to-business and business-to-consumer commerce. International Data Corporation (IDC) <http://www.idcresearch.com/> predicts that electronic commerce in the UK will be driven by businesses selling to businesses. You may decide to go for a fully interactive commerce site linked to a database, with built in added-value functionality such as real-time booking facilities and order tracking. Or you may decide to go for a static site which simply offers information about your products or services with a print and fax order form.

Which option you go for will very much depend on how well prepared your organisation is, which will determine how many extra resources you will need to deploy for each option.

Benefits of selling over the Internet

The main benefits of conducting commerce over the Internet are:

○ *Speed* Electronic commerce speeds up many of the processes involved in the sales cycle, such as, from the consumer's point of view, gathering information on products and services and from the seller's point of view ordering and providing information on products and services and order fulfilment.

○ *Cost savings* By automating ordering, invoicing and customer services this can greatly reduce paperwork. By providing extensive product and services information and ordering facilities over the Web, this can reduce the burden on sales staff. Even if consumers do not place orders over the Internet, preferring to do so by phone, they will be better educated about products and choices, this reduces the time it takes to make a sale. Organisations can save money by offering order-tracking on the Web, so that customers can themselves check in their own time, where their order has got to without having to call customer services. Shipping specialists UPS < http://www. ups.com > estimates that on-line tracking has reduced calls to their customer services centre by 10, 000 per day.

○ *New customers* Selling over the Internet can open up access to new markets and consumers who may prefer this purchasing channel to others.

○ *Access to global markets* Access to global markets can be good news for small businesses, but can cause problems for multinationals because of differential pricing in regional markets and product availability.

Cotton Oxford <http://www.cottonoxford.co.uk> sells rugby shirts through its rugby themed Web site. So far it has generated new sales as far away as New Zealand and Norway.

*At the **Treehugger Designs** <http://www.treehugger.co.uk> Web site you can design your ideal furniture on-line, cost it and place an order. The site has generated a lot of new interest from the US and Japan.*

O ***24-hour shopping*** The Internet never sleeps, your virtual store is open all day and night to take orders, even though, perhaps, it is not possible to offer round the clock delivery.

Benefits from the consumer's point of view include:

O ***Greater selection of products and services*** On-line stores claim to offer a wider selection of goods and services.

O ***Competitive prices*** On-line stores can offer reduced prices because of the reduced overheads of retailing over the Web. Eagle Star Direct <http://www.eaglestardirect.co.uk/> for example, has launched car insurance at a 15 per cent discount if purchased over the Internet.

O ***Saves time*** Takes less time to shop around and compare prices, and you don't have to pay for parking!

O ***An enhanced shopping experience*** Many on-line stores offer more than products or services. Shopping has for many become a leisure activity in its own right involving sensory stimulus and social interaction. In attempting to recreate this in the on-line world, retailers are offering chat rooms related to products or services and detailed product information (eg. the Treehugger site <http://www. treehugger.co.uk> has a lexicography of furniture design terms to help consumers design their own furniture) whilst removing some of the frustrations of everyday shopping such as crowds.

Fortune City <http://www.fortunecity. com/> is a virtual mall that creates an enhanced on-line shopping environment, with chat rooms, themed areas and there is even a 'dateline diner' where you can meet your perfect partner.

Barriers to selling over the Internet

Whilst Internet shopping has great potential it has been slow to take off. Here are some of the problems that merchants face:

O   *Organisational change* Setting up an electronic commerce site requires significant organisational changes such as improving communications and facilitating information exchange to avoid duplication.

O   *Infrastructure not being ready* There is little point in opening up your on-line storefront offering an extensive range of products to order at the click of a button if your delivery channels are not ready.

O   *Lack of on-line payment solutions* There are few reliable on-line payment methods available at present.

O   *Lack of integration with legacy systems* Avoid the situation where you are displaying out-of-stock goods because your site is not integrated with your stock control databases.

O   *Lack of expertise* According to the KPMG Report on Electronic Commerce, organisations feel that they lack the expertise to implement and exploit the opportunities for selling on the Internet.

O   *Security issues* Security issues are perhaps one of the greatest impediments to selling over the Internet both from the consumer's and the merchant's point of view. They revolve around fears of data interception - especially that of credit card details transferred over the Internet; fraud - or misrepresentation of identity and unauthorised users gaining access to organisations' networks. However, it would be accurate to say that currently the perception of risks is greater than actual risks.

Advances in new technology are resolving many of the current security issues and concerns and the evolution of secure on-line payment methods and the changing demographics of Internet users are also speeding up the growth of on-line shopping.

Channel Conflict

Beware when taking the decision to sell your products and services over the Internet that you are not alienating your traditional distributors and customers. If you are selling physical goods it is important to maintain both traditional and on-line channels, or you may end up being worse off.

Segmentation, where you offer products on-line that are not available elsewhere, is an option if you feel that Internet sales are likely to conflict with traditional sales channels.

What you can sell on the Internet

The biggest potential for growth in Internet shopping is in products and services which obey some or all the following criteria.

○   *That can be ordered, paid for and delivered digitally.* **Software is a good example of this type of product as is any information-based product such as books or digital products such as graphics.**

Software.net <http://software.net> software.net has over 2200 software titles for immediate download from the Internet (and a further 20, 000 available for delivery). It claims to be 'the largest Internet-based electronic software superstore, providing customers with the ability to electronically purchase and download software in a simple and secure on-line environment.'

○   **Where customers do not need to, or wish to, or cannot deal with the seller face to face. For instance where the products have an embarrassment factor, such as condoms. Durex <http://www.durex.com> has set up a fun and informative site aimed at young people with a sex advice clinic, on-line lover screensavers to download, postcards to**

send and competitions to win. No product ordering has been featured as yet but plenty of product information including an animated sequence on how to put on a condom. Disabled Internet users are another prime target market which could benefit from on-line shopping for goods and services of many different kinds.

O   *That can be sampled over the Web such as audio and video products.* Or as in the Pure Fiction <http://www.purefiction.com> site extracts of books which can then be bought over the Internet.

Amazon *<http://www.amazon.com> Claims it is the earth's biggest bookstore with 2.5 million books to choose from. Ordering books is done via a shopping cart. You can search for books by author, title, subject, keyword and ISBN. Orders can only be taken on-line.*

Bookpages *<http://www.bookpages.co.uk> A UK based on-line bookshop.*

An example of *niche market* bookselling on the Internet: the *Charity Internet Bookshop* <http://www.aurelian.co.uk> comes on-line in spring 1998 specialising in books of interest to, or published by, non-profit making organisations worldwide.

CDNow *<http://www.cdnow.com> At this 'the world's largest music store' you can listen to artists' work and read their biographies before making a purchase.*

O   *That do not need to be physically seen or do not have a 'touch and feel' quality, before a purchase decision is made.* However, the Internet may be used to raise public awareness of products that do need to be seen. Electrical consumer goods and computer products are good examples.

Dixons *<http://www.dixons.co.uk> is the first UK major electrical store to set up a site. There are 800 products to choose from. Payment can be made by credit card and Dixons Store Cards, using the SSL protocol. Delivery is next day for orders placed before midday. You can also track the status of your order on-line.*

Gateway 2000 *<http://www.gateway2000.co.uk/>* *Gateway 2000 is a computer retailer that has a Web site where users can build their own custom PC, configure it the way they want, calculate the price and order it on-line. There are over 1 million different configurations with product information, photos and performance data. Credit cards are accepted and transactions are secured using the SSL protocol, but users can choose to have a salesperson call them for this information or select an alternate method of payment. The site also has a technical support area with answers to the most frequently asked technical questions.*

O   ***That are simple to understand, configure and order - and this process can be automated*** Treehugger Designs < http://www .treehugger.co.uk >, referred to previously, has made the ordering process of a seemingly complex product - handmade custom designed furniture - into a relatively painless experience

O   ***That are standardised*** For example, books, as consumers do not need to see the product before purchase to know what to expect

O   ***That appeal to a global audience and can be distributed globally.*** This is equally true for products that appeal to a local audience and can be distributed locally. For instance, fresh food would not be suitable for distribution worldwide but is perfect for local deliveries

Tesco *<http://www.tesco.co.uk/>* *The supermarket chain Tesco is now offering home shopping facilities via the Internet to customers in selected trial areas. Customers obtain special software that allows them to browse more than 20,000 products while off-line, and connect to the Internet when necessary to update prices and send orders. Deliveries are made to local areas only.*

Wine Cellar *<http://www.winecellar.co.uk>* *features over 650 products to buy. It features wine descriptions and cooking tips. Delivery is £7.70 or free with orders over £50. Payment is by telephone and delivery is within 14 days.*

Cooks of Swanton *<http://www.gbdirect.co.uk/food/cooksswanton/>* *sell hand-made continental style chocolates, truffles and pralines produced from*

the finest ingredients. British made, hand packed, finished and delivered by first class post. Orders are taken either by fax or phone, with payments accepted by credit card.

The Fresh Food Company *<http://www.freshfood.co.uk/> sells quality organic foods delivered to your door. Payment is by credit card on-line or the order form can be printed out and sent by fax. The site also has a cookbook section which gives recipe ideas.*

Travel and property are amongst the largest growth areas of shopping on the Web.

The travel industry is a prime candidate for changing over to electronic commerce as electronic booking mechanisms have existed for years and it is a relatively uncomplicated process to integrate these with the Internet. It is possible now to book flights, hotels and holidays directly over the Internet in real time. There are also a number of virtual travel agents appearing on the Web such as Microsoft's Expedia <http://www.expedia.com> and TravelWeb <http://www.travelweb.com>.

Property services on the Web are also expanding with many traditional estate agents now opening shop fronts on the Web. The advantage of these is that they offer more precise and extensive property searches that meet the more closely defined criteria that customers expect.

Property Live *<http://www.propertylive.co.uk> is a new initiative launched by the National Association of Estate Agents. Property Live is a register of UK properties for sale or let. Prospective buyers can search for property according to price, location, number of bedrooms and type of property. Brief details and a photograph of the property are included where available. Once you have selected a property that you are interested in, your details are passed on to the Estate Agent handling that property.*

Measuring sales

When calculating numbers of sales over the Internet care must be taken to record new sales and not displacement sales, where an organisation's existing client base simply transfers purchases to the Internet (although, admittedly, those transferred sales may thereby have been achieved at lower cost).

Virtual Malls

Virtual shopping malls are collections of on-line shops grouped together and usually linked by the ability to click on items from one or more stores and place them in a virtual shopping trolley ready for purchase on leaving the mall.

Some virtual malls are simply a collection of links to other stores' sites. Others are fully integrated transactional commerce sites centred around an active on-line community. Virtual shopping malls promote themselves on their ability to capture 'virtual window shoppers'. They are, however, expensive to join and the benefits to the store owner need to be carefully weighed against the benefits of a well-promoted independent store on the Web.

There are usually several options on offer when joining a mall. If you already have a Web site you pay a joining fee and then a monthly rent to have a link to your site from the mall. Sometimes you pay a commission on any sales you achieve. If you don't have a site, most malls can offer full site creation and hosting on their server for a fee, plus a monthly rent and/or commission on sales.

An advantage of joining a shopping mall is that some offer a built-in central purchasing system.

This means that you do not have to invest in shopping trolley software yourself, but do pay a premium for the privilege of using the shopping mall's system, albeit spread over time.

Purchasers enter the shopping mall and can select any items from any store and pay only once. The mall operators take care of the rest. However, this is only possible when customers enter your store via the mall's address. This may mean that you cannot advertise your store in its own right and have to rely on the mall to market themselves effectively in order to attract traffic to your store. In addition, because processes and transactions are dealt with centrally by the mall owners, it may be harder for you to get marketing statistics or even e-mail addresses from visitors to your store.

Before joining a mall it is worth doing some homework. Find out what volume of traffic the site receives. It is best to obtain these figures from an independent Web auditing company.

Virtual Emporium *<http://www.vemporium.com>* *has a cybercafe promoting its mall and encouraging on-line shopping. It also plans to place advertising cones in Los Angeles' shopping areas to encourage existing customers to shop on the Internet.*

The **London Mall** *<http://www.londonmall.co.uk/>* *is a good example of a UK based virtual shopping mall. Shops include Hamleys Toy Shop, Insurance Mall, Kilgour, French & Stanbury, Washington Tremlett, Bernard Weatherill, Psion PDA's, Orange - Portable phones, Sandisk Flashdisk, Cardhost Pro - adaptor, Langfords - silversmith, Holmes Linnette - Ski Maps and Cartridge Care. It also has links to many of the major UK retailers such as Debenhams and Boots.*

Barclay Square *<http://www.barclaysquare.co.uk/>* *is one of the first UK virtual shopping malls. Shops include Airline Network, Argos, Barclays Bank, Blackwells, BT, Campus, Car Shop, Debenhams, Eurostar, HSS, Innovations, Interflora, Pet Protect, Sainsbury's, Sun Alliance, Toys R Us, Tropical Places and Victoria Wine.*

Fortune City *<http://www.fortunecity.com/>* *Is a unique mall based around city streets and communities which offers more than just shopping facilities and is closer to the traditional 'shopping experience'.*

Partnering

Some on-line retailers are offering partnering deals with other sites to promote their products and services. Partnering involves linking up with a third party supplier, where you receive a percentage of profits on goods or services sold and they deal with order processing and dispatching. For the retailer it is a good way of marketing your Web site and promoting your services.

Pure Fiction *<http://www.purefiction.com>* *and* **Bookpages** *<http://www. bookpages.co.uk>. The Pure Fiction site is devoted to writers and book* *lovers, with chat areas, book previews and reviews and a section for new authors. It has a link to The Internet Bookshop so that users can buy books directly.*

On-line shopping catalogues

Placing your product catalogue on-line makes sense when your product selection and prices change frequently.

Both business-to-business catalogues and consumer catalogues can be implemented on the Web. Business-to-business catalogues have been very successful on the Web.

There are two ways of putting your catalogue on-line. The first is to manually code your catalogue pages in HTML for presentation on your Web site. The disadvantages of this method are that it does not represent data in real-time as it is not linked to the organisation's systems. Also it is very resource-intensive manually to rewrite pages to reflect changes.

The second method is to create a product database including information on products and scanned images of products and link this to your Web page with a search facility on top. The database can be updated and Web pages may then be dynamically generated from it.

Benefits of on-line catalogues

O   **Cost savings** The cost of creating a Web catalogue is much less than the cost of originating and distributing several thousand hardcopy catalogues. Once the original content is created, the incremental cost of distributing more catalogues on-line is zero, unlike traditional marketing strategies where sending 10,000 mailshots costs far more than say, 500. Ordering and administrative overheads are also reduced because consumers are using their own time to order. Further savings are made on staff who would otherwise be part of a telesales operation.

○ *Immediate availability* On-line catalogues are available immediately. There is no waiting for printed catalogues to be dispatched by mail - a process that can take weeks.

○ *More information* Much more information can be included about products on a Web site, including, graphics, sound and multimedia.

○ *Frequently updatable* Product information and new products can be added daily, if required.

Disadvantages of on-line catalogues

Image quality is reduced on the Web and it may be slow to browse through on-line catalogues with a slow connection.

Consumer catalogues are making a slow appearance on the Web, largely due to their dependence on credit card transaction systems for on-line payment. Business-to-business catalogues can rely on existing purchase-order-invoice cycles.

Linking searchable product databases to the Internet

Databases can be integrated with a Web site where users may select product categories via a form, which, when submitted, searches a product database and returns results including ordering facilities and product descriptions matching the uses criteria. This is very useful for handling large quantities of products. The advantage of on-line searchable product catalogues is that users can find relevant products easily.

Auto Trader <http://www.autotrader.co.uk/> has a database of 60,000 cars available for searching, by manufacturer, model and region. You can also see photos of some of the cars.

Exchange and Mart <http://www.exchangeandmart.co.uk/> has a database of 50, 000 cars to search through.

Taking purchase orders over the Internet

Purchase orders can be taken in the following ways over your Web site:

O **Print and fax.** Design a purchase order form on your Web site which customers can then print and fax to the seller.

O **E-mail.** You can take orders for products or services by e-mail from your Web site by having a pointer to your e-mail address (also referred to as a *mailto*) and instructions on how to submit the order.

O **Interactive forms.** The best mechanism for taking orders over the Internet is through the use of interactive forms, enabling customers to purchase products or services directly from your Web site. All necessary order information can be entered by the purchaser, it is then automatically e-mailed to you, or sent to a database, ready to be processed by you. An automatic e-mail message can be sent back to purchasers telling them that the order was received and when to expect the goods or services.

Orders can be linked from the Web and integrated directly with corporate systems such as accounting and inventory, thus reducing the amount of manual handling.

Security is obviously an important issue when linking the Web to internal data systems. This can be solved by using third party software/hardware known as middleware to link data stored on a Web server to legacy systems.

On-line payments

Once the buyer has made a selection of goods the next step is to pay for them. There are several ways of doing this ranging from traditional methods such as paying by credit card over the phone to using electronic cash.

One of the main issues in implementing electronic payment transactions as part of your Web marketing strategy is the question of how these electronic payment systems are going to integrate with your organisation's existing systems. To implement electronic payments systems you will need merchant or commerce server software which interfaces between your Web server and a database, and a gateway to banks and other financial institutions.

If setting up your own commerce server does not sound like an appealing option you could go to an Internet Service Provider who offers hosting and implementation of commercial transaction sites.

Electronic payment systems are still in the developmental stages and there is no clear winner yet. Organisations should either go for the current market leader or support several on-line payment methods.

Electronic cash

Electronic cash systems are being developed for the Internet. Electronic cash currency is simply a string of numbers validated by a digital stamp, issued as a token by a bank or similar institution. The value of the token is debited from your bank account. To pay for goods or services with electronic cash you simply send the merchant the necessary number of tokens. The merchant will then send them to the bank to be exchanged for real money. Transactions are then made using an encryption method to ensure security.

Managing your electronic cash is via software that resembles a virtual wallet.

Purchase via electronic cash is anonymous and transfer of funds is immediate. No on-line authorisation is required, nor subsequent clearance of the transaction, nor billing, nor collection of funds. DigiCash <http://www.digicash.com/> is the only true Internet electronic cash system.

Electronic transactions are extremely cheap to process and can therefore be used for smaller payments (also called 'micropayments') which are expensive via other methods such as cheques or credit cards.

This means that merchants are able to sell very small amounts of information.

Microsoft, <http://www.microsoft.com> for example, offers technical support on a Pay Per Incident (PPI) basis, where customers pay per question.

Barclays <http://www.barclaysquare.com> has introduced Barclaycoin, a micro-payment method based on electronic cash. Barclaycoin can be used to pay for goods and services at their virtual mall Barclaysquare.

First Virtual <http://www.firstvirtual.com/> is an electronic cash alternative that does not involve sending credit card details over the Internet. Registered users are assigned a VirtualPIN number which is transmitted instead of their credit card details over secure, dedicated phone lines. Payments must also be authorised by a confirming e-mail between the buyer and First Virtual. This system offers protection to the consumer against fraud by a merchant, as the merchant does not handle credit card processing. Rather this is done via a trusted third party.

CDnow <http://www.cdnow.com> *currently accepts Ecash and gives details on how to set up an Ecash account.*

Smartcards

Mondex <http://www.mondex.com/> a system developed by a consortium of banks including NatWest and Midland, uses smartcards - credit card sized pieces of plastic with a tiny microprocessor chip embedded in them - to store details of credit availability. You can credit your card with money from your traditional account and use the card to pay for goods and services any place that has a card reader. This card reader could, in the future, be built into consumers' PCs. Authentication is done via encrypted data held on the card's chip which is transmitted to the card reader. Digital signatures could also be stored on the chip.

Secure electronic transaction methods

Credit card transactions over the Web are becoming increasingly popular - although acceptance of credit card transactions across the Internet has been slow because of perceptions of Internet security associated with credit card fraud. According to PBS, 84 per cent of Internet users would buy on-line if security levels were higher. Only five per cent are willing to send their credit card details over the Net.

Whilst data such as credit card details can be intercepted along their journey this is not easy for the casual hacker. Credit card details are more likely to be retrieved once stored on a server. Web browsers and servers now have security measures built into them which make on-line financial transactions more secure.

CDNow <http://www.cdnow.com> on its Web site, reassures customers about the security of credit card transactions over the Internet: *'In a 1996 Washington Post article by Rob Pegoraro, David Medine of the Federal Trade Commission suggested that it is much safer to transmit your credit card number over the Internet than to give it to a waiter at a restaurant or read it aloud over a cordless phone -- two activities that are generally taken for granted as safe. In fact, a spokesperson at AT&T's Universal Card division stated that his company to date had not encountered any cases of credit card numbers being stolen during transmission over the Internet'.*

Encryption

One way of protecting details on the Internet is to encrypt them. Encryption is the process of coding data so that it can only be interpreted by the intended recipient. Data can be encrypted before it is transmitted across the Internet and then decrypted upon reaching its destination.

PGP

PGP (Pretty Good Privacy) is an encryption programme that offers a high level of security for sending data across the Internet. PGP works using two keys, one public and one private. The public key is sent to anyone who you may wish to communicate with securely and is used to encrypt a message before it is sent over the Internet. The private key is used to decrypt the message.

Public key servers exist so that people who wish to communicate with you securely can look up your public key. PGP also enables you to add a tamper proof digital signature to your message thereby authenticating it.

The CDNow <http://www.cdnow.com> site gives details of how to use PGP to transmit credit card information securely via e-mail and gives details of where to find its public key.

Secure Electronic Trading (SET)

Secure Electronic Trading (SET), is a new open standard for handling credit card transactions developed by Mastercard and Visa with GTE, IBM, Microsoft, Netscape, SAIC, Teresa Systems and Verisign and with support from American Express, Discover, JCB and Novus.

It is also a protocol which enables Merchant Servers to verify the identity of buyers and reassure them of the legitimacy of sellers. Encrypted credit card details are passed directly to the bank. The bank system then authorises the transaction and processes the accounting and billing for it.

The Joint Electronic Payments Initiative (JEPI) is a standard for handling payment processing, including the ability to handle more than one payment protocol on a single server.

Just as with electronic payment methods, there is no one secure electronic transaction standard that is taking the lead.

Digital certificates

Digital certificates containing encrypted card number and expiry date are used to identify users and merchants. Certification authorities, such as Verisign, <http://www.verisign.com> issue digital certificates. A SET registered Web site can be identified by the TransAct logo. SET currently only works with credit cards but will eventually cover debit cards and other types of payment.

Digital certificates are currently held on the user's computer's hard disk, though it seems likely that in the future smart cards will emerge as the preferred medium for storing digital certificates.

The entire SET system is based on trust and existing relationships between card brand holders, card issuers and cardholders. Merchants are unable to read card details which are passed on to the acquirer. A financial institution known as an acquirer authenticates users and merchants to each other, verifying that they are who they claim to be.

SSL (Secure Socket Layer)

SSL (Secure Socket Layer), is an existing secure communications technology developed by Netscape Communications which is built into many existing browsers. On-line forms can be encrypted if the submit action is an https:// URL to a SSL server. SSL servers are authenticated by a trusted third party via a digital certificate. Whilst SSL enables encrypted communications between user and merchant, it does not enable authentication. Which is where SET comes in.

You can see the security of a page by looking at the security icon in the bottom-left corner of the Netscape Navigator window and the colourbar across the top of the content area.

Secure documents show a doorkey on a blue background with a blue colourbar. The doorkey has two teeth for top security and one tooth for medium security. Insecure documents show a broken doorkey on a grey background with a grey colourbar. In Microsoft Internet Explorer a secure document is indicated by a closed lock in the lower right hand corner of the browser window.

Bookpages <http://www.bookpages.co.uk> *has a number of payment options available:*

- Secure ordering over the Internet *by credit card using SSL encryption for security.*
- Filling in a form, printing it out and faxing or mailing it, *for those who do not want to send financial information over the Internet*
- Telephone Ordering

It also publishes a statement about security, explaining that SSL security features are available on their server and that they plan to adopt the SET standard when it becomes available. Credit card details are also protected on the server by the security built into Windows NT4. Additionally, all order details are saved in a database which is not connected to the Internet and orders are processed at least once a day and then deleted from the server.

Lands End <http://www.landsend.com>, *a clothes retailer on the Web, goes to a lot of trouble to reassure customers that they have adopted tight security standards for their on-line payments and alerting customers as to the real risks of on-line payment methods.*

Customer support over the Internet

The Internet can also be used to offer customer service and support once you have sold your products or services. You can offer customer support via your Web site in any of the following ways:

O   **Provide an e-mail link from your Web site, which goes directly to the customer services department**

O   **Have a Frequently Asked Questions (FAQ) page which answers commonly asked questions and includes troubleshooting tips**

O   **Provide an e-mail link from your Web page to a call-back facility which links users to the customer services department.**

O   **In the case of some software and hardware companies your Web page can be used to supply updates, fixes and patches.**

The Data Protection Act

British Web sites that collect personal data about their users, including names, addresses and credit card details, to target content and advertising must be registered with the Data Protection Registrar or face fines.

Merchant Server software

Merchant Server software provides the whole range of services which are needed to enable visitors to view and buy merchandise. These services include the ability to display product details held in a separate database, search for products, fill an electronic shopping basket with purchases, process orders, carry out user identification, apply for a credit account, check credit, process secure payments, capture visitor preferences and more.

OpenMarket's Transact <http://www.openmarket.com>, IBM's NetCommerce <http://www.uk.ibm.com> and Microsoft's Commerce Server <http://www.microsoft.com> are three examples. Most Merchant Server software uses a shopping trolley metaphor, where users browse the Web site selecting purchases and adding them to their shopping trolley. The user can at any time view the contents of the trolley and add or delete any items.

Summary

O   The Internet can be used to provide information about products and services, to purchase and pay for goods and services, to distribute certain products and services and offer customer support and service.

O   Selling and buying over the Internet is becoming increasingly popular and is set to play a very important role in the future.

O   The main barriers to selling over the Internet concern perceptions of lack of security and available on-line payment methods.

O   Travel, property, books, CDs and software are the most popular products available to buy on the Internet.

O   An alternative to setting up your own commercial Web site is to join a virtual shopping mall and let them design your storefront and process your transactions.

O   On-line catalogues are an efficient way of presenting large quantities of products that change often.

O   Electronic payment systems are still under development and include electronic cash and smartcards.

O   Security of on-line payment transactions is guaranteed by two standards - SSL and SET.

O   Encryption and digital certificates - features of on-line payment systems - help protect data and identify users.

O   Customer support and services can be offered from your site, completing the product sales cycle on the Internet.

7 Marketing on the Web

The most common and powerful part of the Internet for marketing is the World Wide Web.

Why use the Web for marketing?

○ *It is cost effective* Marketing on the Web is inexpensive compared to traditional marketing methods. One obvious cost saving is made on the distribution and printing costs of large glossy product brochures.

○ *It is worldwide* The Web offers your marketing campaign access to a global audience and marketplace.

○ *It has a broad and diverse user base enabling access to new markets* The Internet today has progressed from being a haven for academics and computer buffs to an important resource for business and for a wide range of non-profit activities. Since the development of the Web, an increasing number of organisations and individuals from different disciplines and commercial sectors have been using the Internet as a reliable source and exchange forum for information.

○ *It is frequently and easily updatable* Web pages can be updated daily, if necessary, offering higher levels of topicality. This is especially useful if you are publishing information that changes frequently or for an audience that requires up-to-date information. A travel company offering holidays confronts the constant problem of flight times, prices and availability changing at the last minute - it is costly to update these in a printed brochure but very easy and cheap to make changes on the Web site, ensuring that holidaymakers have the latest available information at their fingertips.

○ *It enables feedback and direct response* Interactive forms and direct e-mail responses from a Web site promote new forms of dialogue with 'virtual stakeholders'.

Interactive Web pages can be used for customer support services, selling and payment transactions as well as market research.

Cisco <http://www.cisco.com>, *a networking equipment company, has achieved 20 per cent productivity-gain through Internet-based initiatives such as switching customer service and support to the Internet, saving on head-count, while maintaining or improving customer satisfaction.*

Customer orders are increasingly placed interactively over the Internet. 16% of Cisco's orders now come via the net, up from zero a year ago. (July 1997)

○ *It enables you to identify audiences and build user profiles* Via usage statistics on your site you can determine who is accessing your Web site, what they are accessing and when.

○ You can learn a great deal about your customers and build up a picture of who they are and what their needs are from their activities on the Web by the use of cookies (see Chapter 4) and interactive forms.

○ *It offers exciting new ways to present information* Video and sound can be accessed over the Web. New developments such as Java are making the Web more interactive, enabling real time data feeds to be built into your Web pages. You can also access files and databases over the Web. Information presented in an unusual way will bring increased customer visits to your Web site.

○ *It is an efficient way of storing and retrieving information* Information on the Web is instantly and permanently accessible, and takes up no storage space. Archives of information can easily be made available. The task of tracking down relevant information is much simpler with the help of Internet search tools. Information retrieved from the Web can be downloaded directly for use.

○ *It is an inexpensive way of presenting specific information to individual target markets* Publishing on the Web can make provision of tailored information to individual stakeholder groups more affordable. The Web has a great capacity for highly targeted marketing or 'narrowcasting' as it is known.

What makes the Web different from other marketing media?

○ It is not time-restricted - users can access the Web at any time of day or night.

○ It is interactive - users can interact (ie. talk back) on Web pages. At its simplest, interactivity involves filling in forms and getting a response by either e-mail or on the Web page. However, new technologies such as Java and VRML mean that more sophisticated, and so more appealing, levels of interactivity, are possible, such as real-time chat on Web pages.

○ It is non-linear - this means that users can jump from the middle of one page to another and then back, and then perhaps to a third page, and so on. Users can be guided by you but ultimately they can choose what they see of your site, how much and in what order.

○ It is multimedia - Web sites can include graphics, audio, video and animation.

○ It is screen-based - Web sites are viewed on a computer. Computer screen sizes vary but they are generally wider and shorter than an A4 page. Web marketers must stop thinking in terms of the high quality graphics and A4 pages of brochure or magazine publications. Screen-based graphics are lower quality than print-based graphics and a photo from a glossy brochure may not translate well to a Web page.

O It is dynamic - Web sites must be continuously up-dated to attract return visits from users. Always remember that users expect your site to be up to date, if it is not then you fall short of their expectations - which does not reflect well upon what you are trying to market.

O It requires active retrieval - the Web is a user-selected medium. Users choose to go to a particular Web site. You may not necessarily choose to view an advert in a cinema but if you wanted to see that same advert on the Web you would have to choose to do so actively.

Those features that are particular to the medium mean that it is not appropriate for all types of data. For instance, it is not suitable for text-heavy content, but it does lend itself well to graphical presentation. The Web catches people's imagination because it can display multimedia (sound, graphics and video). However, care must be taken when using multimedia-rich presentations not to exclude low bandwidth users.

Often Web site content does not take advantage of the inherent capabilities of the Internet, such as interactivity. Many sites simply present a massive amount of static, text-heavy organisational information.

Before embarking on a Web marketing strategy, get to know the medium as a user and discover for yourself what it has to offer, and what the effect of the various technologies are upon you as a user. Book yourself on an introductory Internet course or pick up one of the numerous books on the subject to familiarise yourself with how the Web works. Spend some time browsing the Web looking at other sites. Check out what others in your sector are doing. The key to marketing success on the Web is to think of the medium in its own terms and not simply to apply the same rules as for traditional marketing media.

The biggest mistake is to think of the Web as some cheap form of print.

Types of marketing Web site

There are three main types of marketing Web site:

○ **Promotional Web sites - these contain background information on the company, information about products and recent press releases. They can also be used on an Intranet to distribute information to marketing personnel.**

○ **Content-based Web sites - these provide timely information, which is regularly updated.**

○ **Transactional Web sites - these enable Internet users to purchase products, view product information and engage customer support.**

Key stages in developing a marketing Web site

Once you have answers to the following questions, you are ready to start thinking about the content, layout and look of your Web site.

○ **Is the Web an appropriate marketing medium for your organisation?**

○ **Can your target markets be reached via the Web and what are their needs?**

○ **What are the aims and objectives of your Web site?**

See Chapter 2 for further details on how to answer these questions.

Stage one: building content

Content should be user- and not company-driven. A successful Web site is designed with the user's requirements in mind and not just as a place to display cutting edge technologies. You should have in front of you a list of desired content, defined by users.

Editorial content

Bearing in mind that the Web is not suitable for text-heavy content, you will need to edit any text that you wish to include in your Web site so that it is concise and 'bite sized'. There is nothing that will put people off your Web site more than having to scroll through numerous pages of dense text.

If you *must* present large amounts of text you may consider:

○ **breaking the text up into several linked pages, or one long page with a menu at the top and links to each section of the page. This has the advantage of being printable in one go should viewers prefer.**

○ **breaking the text up visually with the use of lists, bullets, horizontal rules.**

○ **saving the text in a format such as Adobe Acrobat, and making it available to download from your site - including a link to download the Adobe Acrobat Viewer for people to be able to view your document.**

It is worth getting someone with editorial skills to write text for you. The Internet is a relaxed medium; communications are less formal and more conversational in style. The tone of your editorial should reflect this.

Multimedia content

Multimedia - graphics, sound and video - is the most visible aspect of a Web site and adds to the Web experience. But it does not always add to the site's ability to meet organisational objectives and, indeed, may limit the audience to high bandwidth users. Think carefully about whether your multimedia content ties in with the aims and objectives of the site before including them.

Using advanced technologies can be expensive. You also need to determine whether your audience will be able to use those features - at present, few can.

Graphics

Many Web sites detract from their marketing message because of poor use of images. In order to ensure that your images work for your Web site and not against it:

○ **think about whether the image adds to the site**
○ **use colour, logos and images for branding**
○ **choose a Web graphic designer who understands Web graphic file formats**
○ **keep images small**
○ **it is good practice to include a text alternative to your image - 15% of users with graphic viewing capabilities switch these off and 5% of users have text-only Browsers such as Lynx. In addition the text alternative will be displayed whilst the image is downloading, giving users an idea of what they are about to see.**
○ **try not to put too many images on one page because the Browser has to open a connection for each image, which takes time.**
○ **most Browsers will cache images ie. they will store the image in memory. If that image is needed again it does not then need to be downloaded from the Server once more, but is simply retrieved from your computer's hard disk. It is a good idea to try and use the same image over more than one page. This will speed up your Web pages.**
○ **try to keep the total size of all images on one page to under 50k.**
○ **if your site uses different coloured backgrounds make sure that any text that goes in front of this ground is still completely legible.**
○ **if you are using a background image, make sure that the file is not too large, otherwise it may take a while to download.**

Interactivity

Adding interactivity in marketing terms shifts the onus of control onto the user. With a highly interactive site they make the choices and this can be a very engaging experience. However, you may not always want to give your audience that much control.

If you want to promote your product or organisation via the Web you may want to guide them precisely through each stage of the sales cycle. Whereas if your aim is to attract traffic for advertisers you may need to give users full control as they move through the site. How interactive you make the site depends on the aims and objectives you have set for the site to achieve.

The Mini <http://www.mini.co.uk> site is a good example of interaction based around their current advertising campaign. You can design your own mini on the site and there is a prize for the best design with a gallery of other people's designs.

Managing response

Interactivity is a two way thing - an important part of building interactivity into your Web site is the response mechanism. You will need to put in place the proper resources to answer queries and to set realistic targets and expectations with regard to response times.

One method of automating responses from a Web site is to use an infobot or autoresponder. This is an automated e-mail message that is directed to anyone who sends a message to a particular address - providing instant feedback from your site.

They can be used for people sending messages to the Webmaster or contacts, or to thank visitors and give realistic response time expectations.

Planning your Web site

Once you have established what it is you want to put on your Web pages, the next step is to think about how you are going to organise the content.

The home page is usually the starting point of your site. This 'typically' contains information about the content of the site. Sometimes you may come across a 'splash page', which serves as an introduction and usually consists simply of a graphic feature that you click on to get to the contents page.

Remember that users may come into your site at any point. Therefore it is important to ensure that each page in your site links to your home page and provides enough contextual information for users to identify the page with your organisation.

You can have as many pages as you like in your Web site. Bear in mind however, that, the more pages you have, the more complicated it is to maintain the links subsequently and the easier it is for a browser to get 'lost' in your Web scheme.

Page Length

One final consideration before you decide how you are going to structure your content is to decide how big to make each page. The larger the page, the longer it will take to transfer and, therefore, the harder it will be to navigate from one page to another. Also, it is difficult to navigate or scroll through a page that is too long.

The general rule is to try to make menu pages or home pages not much larger than a full screen, and textual material not greater than A4 - and broken up wherever possible.

Navigation

Most of your users are accustomed only to using the traditional linear development of the printed media (where page 58 is followed by page 59 and there are few choices to be made). The ability to move in many different directions and the atmosphere of constant choice and selection can be disorientating rather than exciting.

Disorientation is not a state that will make the viewer receptive to your marketing message.

Some sites consist of thousands of pages. For the novice user, this can be a bit daunting to navigate. If navigation is done well, users will glide through your site and be able to find what they are looking for.

If done badly, you can guarantee that users will leave quickly and not return.

Navigation is, perhaps, one of the most powerful tools that the Web marketer has. You have almost complete control over where users go. If you have not provided a link to a page then they cannot get there easily. If you wish to lead the consumer through a product sales cycle, from product information to ordering and payment, you simply provide the right options. Here are some tips on improving the quality of navigation through your site:

○ provide a menu of navigation options, including a link back to the home page, throughout your Web pages to make browsing through your site easier at all points.

○ *enmeshing* refers to the practice of creating links to other pages *within your own* Web site. It is important to incorporate navigation bars on all your Web pages, clearly spelling out all the link options to pages within your site. It means that users do not have to keep going back to the home page to get deeper into your site. You can have them either as text or as pictures, or both.

○ make navigational icons consistent throughout your site, so that users get used to which icon does what. If you have used buttons with blue text and a red background to indicate a link to another page, do not suddenly start using buttons with red text on a blue background.

○ let people know where they are in relation to the rest of the site. One way of doing this is to use a menu with the relevant menu item highlighted while the user is in the document corresponding to that item. Another way is to use a site map at the bottom of the page which displays a visual representation of the site with the location of the current page clearly marked on it. Site maps are also a good idea to let people know what else is on the site and where.

○ if you are including a long page with anchor links from a menu at the top, it is a good idea to place navigational links back to the top of the page.

○ building a search engine into your site will help users to locate information effectively, especially if there is a lot of information on the site.

○ if the main objective of your site is to sell products, then all pages should have a link to a product order form.

Attracting traffic to your site

Establish a dialogue with your stakeholders

It is a mistake to think that people will seek out a Web site simply for information about a company or advertising. Marketing on the Web is about establishing an entirely new relationship with stakeholders, creating more of a continuing dialogue that will have people coming back again and again. Part of maintaining a dialogue with your stakeholders includes providing value-added content, something that will make users come back.

The greatest marketing opportunity occurs on users' first visit to your site - once users have left they may never return. The best marketing strategy is to convert visits into an ongoing dialogue.

One-to-One marketing

One of the great advantages of marketing on the Web is that you can market to quite specific target markets and deliver appropriate marketing messages right down to an individual consumer. Web pages can present tailored information - if a user accesses a particular type of information the page can be programmed to present other, similar, information. Or customised pages can be created based on a single customer's defined criteria

Value Added marketing

The Internet is widely used for information and entertainment. In fact, a new term has been coined to describe entertainment such as games and puzzles which are also informative or educational - 'infotainment' or 'edutainment'.

People often visit a Web site for free information; they are not planning to buy products or services or read organisational literature or look at adverts. Although, obviously, that is what you will encourage them to do once they arrive on your site. Virtually all successful Web sites offer some information of value or entertainment, free of charge.

Cheestrings <http://www.cheestrings.co.uk> *The Cheestrings site offers interactive games which are very engaging and appeal to kids - their target market.*

Examples of free information includes newsletters, free downloadable demos of software, advice shops and e-zines, pictures or photographs, screensavers, and links to other useful sites. A bank may, for instance, offer a free mortgage calculator. This will be of interest to home owners or first time buyers - the bank's target market. A travel agent may offer travel tips.

Even virtual postcards, which tend to multiply around Christmas, are an appealing free 'gift' which also promotes your organisation. These are postcard shaped images which you can e-mail to friends with your own message. The Terrence Higgins Trust <http://www.tht.org.uk> site, for example, has postcards mirroring its real life postcards helping raise AIDS awareness. The Mini <http://www.mini.co.uk> site has 4 postcards that you can send to friends which represent images from their latest advertising campaign. The postcards are very colourful and feature a mini in them - promoting minis as hip and trendy. Free product or service samples can be offered on a time-limited basis to encourage swift purchase action on the part of the visitor.

Abbey National <http://www.abbeynational.co.uk> *This site is an example of a Web site offering value-added content. It has a section on managing your money which includes a mortgage calculator that works out how much various loans will cost you. Further information can be requested via an e-mail form. Content is topical with features on current issues relevant to the homebuyer such as negative equity. The site also has a Prize Draw, with Marks & Spencer vouchers as prizes. This feature enables Abbey National to compile names of site users for possible leads.*

Be Unique

You can be unique by:

- offering a unique product or service over the Net
- having a unique Web site
- using a new technology
- being the first in your business sector to be on the Web

New developments in Web and Internet technologies mean that creating a unique Web site is becoming easier. Your site will be talked about and will receive press coverage - thus increasing the traffic. People will come to your site just to see the latest technologies or unique form of presentation. Guinness <http://www.guinness.com> achieved this by being one of the first sites to offer a downloadable screensaver. Even the Spice Girls pages achieved some notoriety for being one of the first Web sites to showcase the potential of Quark's Immedia software.

Design Considerations

Creating an informative and effective site for maximum communication potential must incorporate the following features:

O *Consistency* Be consistent throughout your site with respect to font sizes and headings, general page layout and style. This will provide your site with a strong organisational identity and users will recognise wherever they are that they are in your site. An effective way of implementing consistency is to use the same borders, bullets, backgrounds, logos, themes and colours throughout.

O *Accessibility* The longer users have to wait to download your site the more likely it is that they will move on. It is therefore to your advantage to ensure that your pages do not contain too much bandwidth-consuming multimedia. In addition, it is helpful to have a version of your site available for people to download from your site to browse off-line, and to have print outs of the site available for those who do not have access to the Internet. Provide alternatives to graphics and non-standard features such as frames. If you want accessibility for the largest number of users, or if your target users are known to be low bandwidth users, design your Web pages to the lowest common denominator.

O *Readability* Use short paragraphs, lists and horizontal rules to break up long pieces of text. Even better, avoid long chunks altogether with careful editing.

○ *Simplicity* Avoid overcrowding your pages and creating what in Net jargon is called *an angry fruit salad.*

○ *Look and Feel* Use writing style, font style, colour, graphics and advanced technologies to give your Web site character.

While working on the design of your Web pages, you should consider at all times how each page ties into your marketing strategy and objectives.

Link strategies

The ability to have hypertext documents linked together is a powerful feature of the Web.

Linking extensively to other sites has the benefit of increasing traffic to your site by providing a valuable service to users. It does, however, have the disadvantages of increasing the likelihood of you losing visitors to other Web sites and the cost and time of maintaining links. You may become more of a road than a destination.

If you do want to provide links to other sites, ask yourself if this fits in with your marketing aims and objectives.

To avoid losing visitors to other sites too quickly:

○ 'bury' your link page towards the lower echelons of your Web site

○ provide clear but not too enticing link buttons/text out of your site

○ do not provide links to other sites on your home page - otherwise you will find visitors are not even stopping to browse any of your site.

Other links you might like to make are to browsers, plug-ins and other useful software that will enhance users' experience of viewing your site. Links to positive press notices and awards on your site are good for publicity.

Meeting the needs of the global community

It is important to remember that the Web has global reach. If your intended audience is not worldwide it is good practice to clearly spell out your geographical capabilities ie. stating that your products or services are available only in certain regions.

If your intended audience is worldwide it is a good idea to:

O   **Translate your pages into multiple languages and be able to handle native language enquiries**
O   **Provide multinational content. For example, when using interactive forms and questionnaires bear in mind that not all countries use postcodes**
O   **Provide international phone numbers such as (44 181) 960 7918**
O   **Price products in local currency**
O   **Provide e-mail contact for out of hours**

Stage two: building your Web site

Once you have your content and structure the next stage is actually building your Web site. Your two options include:

O   **Building the site in-house**
O   **Out-sourcing to an independent Web designer**

Building the site in-house

World Wide Web pages are created using a set of commands that describe how a document is to be formatted and displayed. This code is called HyperText Markup Language (HTML) and uses tags to format text, include graphics and make links to other pages.

To familiarise yourself with what HTML looks like and to pick up a few hints and tips it is a good idea to have a look at some examples of pages on the

Web. Most Browsers have the capability of showing you the HTML scripting for the current page.

There are various flavours of HTML. HTML 3.2 is the current standard of HTML. Netscape, impatient with waiting for new standards to be agreed, brought out some extensions to HTML of its own which are not yet supported by all Browsers. Microsoft have also brought out their own extensions. If a tag is not supported by a Browser it will just ignore it.

When you are writing your Web pages you will have to decide whether or not you want to use HTML extensions that are not supported by all Browsers. From a marketing point of view this will depend on what Browser your target audience is using. A way around this would be to provide alternative pages that are interpreted by all Browsers. If you design pages with a particular Browser in mind, mention on your Home Page that the pages are best viewed with that Browser and you could provide a link to download that Browser.

Learning HTML

HTML is a simple language to learn. There are a number of computer training companies that offer HTML courses, including The Web Factory <http://www.webfactory.co.uk> 01782-858585, World Wide Web Services Ltd <http://www.webs.co.uk> 01784-466555, Happy Computers <http://www.happy.co.uk> 0171-278 5596, The Internet Training Centre <http://www.internet-training.co.uk/> 0171-355 1270 and UUNET PIPEX <http://www.pipex.com> 01223-250100.

O   **Most cybercafes also offer Web authoring courses.**

There are also a number of good teach yourself HTML books available. One of the best ones is Laura Lemay's *Teach Yourself Web Publishing in a Week*, published by Sams Net <http://www.lne.com/Web/HTML/index.html>.

There are also many helpful resources on-line including:

O   *NCSA's Beginner's Guide to HTML* < http://www.ncsa.uiuc. edu/General/Internet/WWW/HTMLPrimer.html >
O   *Yale Web Style Guide*
      < http://info.med.yale.edu/caim/manual/ >

O *Introduction to HTML* < http://www.cwru.edu/help
/introHTML/toc.html >

The tools of the trade

Web pages can be created using any text editor such as Notepad - the text
editor that comes with Windows - or any Word Processing package.

HTML editors

HTML editors are tailor-made software specially made for authoring Web
pages and incorporating shortcut features and buttons that enable you to create
HTML documents without having to remember every HTML command.

There are special HTML editors available which include short-cut buttons and
features to writing HTML. Some also provide WYSIWYG (What You See is
What You Get) capabilities.

Some popular HTML editors include:

SoftQuad HoTMetaL Pro: <http://www.softquad.com>
HTML Assistant Pro: <http://www.brooknorth.com>
Hot Dog Pro: <http://www.fourthnet.co.uk/hotdog>

A step up from HTML editors are WYSIWYG editors with site management
tools built in:

Microsoft FrontPage 97: <http://www.microsoft.com/>
Adobe PageMill: <http://www.adobe.com>
Net Objects Fusion <http://www.netobjects.com>

HTML filters and converters

There are also HTML filters available that will convert the output from Word-
processors, spreadsheets and databases into HTML. These are available for
many software applications including Microsoft Word 6 for Windows,

Microsoft Access and Microsoft Excel. These are useful for converting existing documents on to the Web as fast as possible. They are less flexible than HTML editors, especially when it comes to links and images and fancy features such as Frames. You will still need a knowledge of HTML as you will inevitably have to do some editing and manipulating of HTML when maintaining your Web pages.

HTML editors and filters are limited as they do not stay current with the latest releases of HTML, which means that you cannot take advantage of new HTML features until your editor or filter catches up. Also HTML editors and filters can create very inefficient and sometimes incorrect HTML.

Choosing a Web designer to author your site

It may be that you do not have the skills, resources or time to build your own Web pages. There are numerous Web design companies and individual designers who can take your project to completion.

A good Web designer should:

O   **Be able to interpret your needs**
O   **Not be either technology or design led, but a combination of both with strong marketing abilities**
O   **have the necessary skills and equipment for the job - building Web sites involves the use of high end machines and often requires programming skills**
O   **focus on needs rather than technology tricks**

Where to find a Web designer

On-line directories:
http://www.yacc.co.uk/britind/internet.html
http://www.ukdirectory.com/computer/ser.htm
http://www.webdesign.co.uk/
http://www.internet-directory.co.uk

Internet Service Providers:
Most Internet Service Providers offer basic Web design consultancy.

Freelance Web Producers:
Many graphic design graduates and undergraduates offer freelance Web production. Ring your local college to enquire.

Media agencies:
There are plenty who are dealing with the Internet eg.
Megalomedia <http://www.megalomedia.com> 0171-447 5599

Graphic design houses:
Many traditional graphic design houses also offer Web production facilities.

Web design houses:
The Web Factory <http://www.webfactory.co.uk > 01782-858585
AKQA <http://www.akqa.co.uk> 0171-823 9333
Arawak Interactive Marketing <http://www.arawak.co.uk>
Bluewave <http://www.bluewave.co.uk/> 0171-706 3500
Domino Systems <http://www.domino.com> 01865-391111
NoHo Digital <http://www.noho.co.uk> 0171- 299 3434
On-line Magic <http://www.onlinemagic.com/online/> 0171- 820 7766
Webmedia <http://www.webmedia.co.uk> 0171-224 7244

When sourcing a Web designer ask for the following:

- **examples of work and the company's own Web site**
- **ask the company to suggest some of their clients that you may ring up and discuss how well they worked together**
- **ask whether the company has done any other Web sites for your business sector**
- **ask whether they have any specialisations ie. database integration, on-line shopping, etc.**

Get as much information as you can from each company. Then draw up a shortlist of 3 to 4 designers and invite them to make a pitch.

Be prepared

When briefing designers for a Web site, make sure that you have done your homework and that you are clear about the aims and objectives of the site, about your target audience, and have some ideas about content - how you would like to see the layout and structure and which features, such as feedback forms, you would like included.

Costs

Expect to start talking figures once you have given designers your brief and discussed it with them. They should then have a good idea of what you want, and be able to quote accordingly.

Many companies offer starter packs for under £1000 which, typically, include a fixed number of pages and graphics, and a few additional features such as mailtos, counters and linking to search engines. With this type of deal you are expected to provide text and graphics yourself, as the fee is unlikely to include designing graphics and writing editorial content - a good option if you just want to dip a toe in the water, but do not expect a marketing miracle.

Further up the scale are larger sites which focus on the type of Web site rather than the exact number of pages and graphics. For example, a product brochure with ordering facilities or a fully-featured large marketing Web site - these often include graphic design, interactivity and back-end databases.

By the second stage you should expect a quote and a written spec for the site. Does the quote include maintenance, domain name registration and hosting? Will they train you or your staff to manage and maintain the site?

The contract

You should draw up a contract with agreements in writing including a timescale for the project, penalty clauses and incentives for meeting targets - and any guarantees should you be completely dissatisfied with the implementation of your brief. You should also agree on who owns the copyright of material.

Testing your site

To make sure your information will look good to a very wide audience, you should test your pages on as many Browsers as possible running on as many different platforms. The minimum would be to test your pages for Netscape Navigator 2, MS Internet Explorer 2 and NCSA Mosaic running on at least Windows and, if possible, UNIX and Mac systems.

It is often a good idea to set up a usability group of end users to try out your pages and note where they experience difficulty, whether that is in trying to navigate your site or in finding information on your site.

Stage three: putting your Web site on to the Internet

Once your Web site is ready, the next stage is to transfer it onto a Web Server - a computer permanently connected to the Internet running special software which deals with requests for your Web pages.

You can either set up your own Web Server or rent space on an Internet Service Provider's (ISP) Web Server. The latter is the cheaper alternative.

Setting up your own Web Server

To set up your own Web Server you will need:

O   a dedicated machine and a fast permanent high bandwidth connection to the Internet
O   Web Server software that sits on your computer.
O   The two most popular Web Server platforms are Microsoft Windows NT and Unix. The choices of server software are between Apache (Unix based) Microsoft's Internet Information Server, Netscape's range of servers and Novell's Web Server. There are two good public domain Web Servers: CERN's HTTPD <http://www.w3.org/Servers> HTTPD <http://hoohoo.ncsa.uiuc.edu/docs/overview.html>, from NCSA, available for most platforms.
O   A Webmaster with knowledge of UNIX, cgi scripting and Internet security.

Setting up your own Server is very expensive and resource intensive.

Choosing an ISP to host your site

A fast and reliable Internet Service Provider (ISP) to host your site is crucial. The more unstable your site the more discontented users you will have. You may lose sales, for example, if users are continuously unable to access your site. Consider the following when choosing an ISP to host your site:

❑ **Choose an ISP with fast links to the Internet from their Web server and a reliable connection.**

❑ **Find out how much traffic they have to their Web server and whether they will charge you extra if your Web site generates a large amount of traffic (sometimes referred to as *throughput*).**

❑ **Find out whether they provide any free Web space - most do - and how much they charge for extra space. Charges are based on storage, typically per megabyte per month. Expect to pay around £25 per month for 5MB.**

❑ **Do they provide Web page access to formatted statistical reports?**

❑ **Do they allow forms handling scripts on their servers? CGI (Common Gateway Interface) scripts also known as PERL scripts, enable users to interact with your Web pages. For instance, to fill in a questionnaire or search for something on your Web pages. Building these capabilities requires an element of programming and may not be for the faint hearted. Not all Internet Service Providers (ISPs) will allow you to run gateway scripts that you have written yourself on their Web Servers for security reasons. Some ISPs will have standard scripts for you to build into your pages.**

❑ **Find out if your ISP can handle secure transactions on your behalf and whether there is an extra charge for this.**

❑ **What methods does your ISP allow you to use to update your Web pages? Ftp access to a server enables a greater degree of control and flexibility in when, and how often, you can update your pages. Some ISPs do not allow you to access files directly on their servers and prefer you to e-mail your files to them. Some ISPs charge extra to do this if they offer ftp access as well, others restrict the number of times they allow you to update your pages by this** method. Some ISPs allow you to update your pages over the Web.

○ Check whether they have an adequate number of phone lines and powerful enough computers. They should also have a back up server and power generator in case either the server or power goes down. Think of the bad publicity if your site is frequently off-line because of inadequate equipment and facilities.

○ Ensure that they have proper security measures in place on their Web servers. For example, passwords should be encrypted and stored on a separate server not connected to the Internet.

Register your domain name

A domain name is a unique alphanumeric address that points to a location such as a Web site, on the Internet. An example of a domain name is: acompany.co.uk It forms an important part of your Web site address eg. http://www.acompany.co.uk and, as such, plays an important part in your organisational identity.

acompany.co.**uk**

There are three levels in a domain name. The top-level domain (the two letters to the far right in the above example) identifies the country - in this case the UK. US addresses do not include a top-level domain.

acompany.**co**.uk

The next level indicates the type of organisation.
.co is a commercial company. The equivalent in the US is .com
.org is a not-for-profit organisation
.ac is an academic institution. The equivalent in the US is .edu
Some new domains are in the process of being added which include .plc and .ltd for UK companies registered at Companies House.

acompany.co.uk
The third part is chosen by you and can be up to 63 characters.

Anyone can register a domain name through NomiNet - the UK non-profit organisation responsible for administering .uk domains. NomiNet charges £50 a year to administer a domain name.

Or a cheaper alternative is to register either with a service provider or one of the number of companies who specialise in selling domain names as they offer up to 40% discount on NomiNet fees.

Companies who specialise in selling domain names include:

The Web Factory <http://www.webfactory.co.uk>
Names.co <http://www.names.co.uk>
NetBenefit <http://www.domainnames.co.uk/>
NetNames <http://www.netnames.co.uk/>
WorldWide Web Services <http://www.webs.co.uk>

When choosing domain names it is a good idea to:

- register them for all the countries that your organisation has a presence in
- register them for all brand names, generic words and trademarks owned by, or associated with, your organisation eg. the National Asthma Campaign might register the domain asthma.org.uk
- choose an intuitive name: many users search for sites by guessing the URL
- register more than one possibility and point those addresses to one site.

Protecting your Web site

You will need to think about protecting your Web site from:

- tampering
- deletion or removal

If your Web site is installed on a Web server on your organisation's network, protecting your Web site is a simple case of installing a firewall in front of your server.

A firewall is a piece of software that sits on a machine and acts as a gatekeeper, controlling access in and out of the network.

If you are renting space on a server however, it is a little harder to control security. The greatest security risk from rented space concerns the storage of the passwords that enable you to access your Web site.

These are often stored on the ftp server and should be adequately encrypted.

Copyright

The Internet is something of a minefield where copyright is concerned. With so much content freely available on the Net, it is very tempting to just lift it and use it in your Web pages. This is not recommended unless you have obtained explicit permission from the author. Otherwise you are liable to find yourself facing legal action.

As far as copyrighting your own work is concerned, it is a good idea to include a copyright statement on your Web page. This can be done by linking a copyright statement to a button on your Home Page. Bear in mind, however, that, potentially, material can be copied and used anywhere in the world.

Technologies are being developed that will allow material to be viewed on the Web but not downloaded unless a small payment is made. Copyright protection laws are also being adapted to cover electronic data.

Stage four: marketing your Web pages

Once you have painstakingly built your Web pages and found a home for them on a server, the next step is to tell the world about them. Publishing information on the Web is no guarantee that anyone will visit or even know where it is.

It is not necessary to market your Web pages continuously as they change, but it is, perhaps, a good idea to let people know of important new content or features on your site.

There are many ways to let the world know about your site. These include announcements on the Internet itself, through traditional media and via your organisation's communications.

The first thing to do is write a press release which outlines the aims and objectives of the site, what can be found on it, what to expect from it in the future and, perhaps, include some screen shots of the site.

The following is an example of a press release issued by The International Fund Raising Group <http://www.ifrg.org.uk> when it launched its Web site in 1996.

PRESS RELEASE

*The **International Fund Raising Group (IFRG)** successfully launched its Web site recently. It can be located at: http://www.ifrg.org.uk. The Group will use the site to reach out to fundraisers and managers of non-profit organisations worldwide with an interest in fundraising. "We embrace the Internet as an integral part of our communication with a truly worldwide audience" says Per Stenbeck, Chief Executive of the Group. "Every year some 3000 fundraisers from more than 100 countries attend the International Fund Raising Workshop and the regional workshops on fundraising we help organise each year in Africa, Asia, Latin America and Eastern Europe."*

The IFRG has opted for a clean, easy-to-use approach which pays particular attention to content over bandwidth-consuming technologies aimed as it is at a worldwide base of users a large share of whom have low bandwidth access to the Internet.

The site carries:

- *general information about the International Fund Raising Group, its history and its governing structure.*
- *information about the up-coming International Fund Raising Workshop in October in Holland every year with full details of all sessions and speakers as well as a registration form.*
- *regular updates on the regional workshops in Africa, Asia, Latin America and Eastern Europe with latest news on dates, places and local points of contact.*

- *information about the IFRG training courses in fundraising and how to organise them.*
- *information about 'The Worldwide Fundraisers' Handbook' and how to order it.*

The International Fund Raising Group is a non-profit organisation promoting ethical fundraising worldwide. For further details please contact: International Fund Raising Group, 295 Kennington Rd, London SE11 4QE Tel: +44 0171-587 0287 Fax: +44 0171-582 4335 ho27@dial.pipex.com

Understand how visitors find your Web site

It is impossible to determine the source of users who simply type in your URL, although it is known that these tend to come from more traditional reference sources such as magazines. It is also difficult to track the number of people who have found your site as a direct result of specific marketing campaigns you have launched. The results of a survey detailing the most common ways in which people find Web sites is available at <http://www.usnews.com/>.

The survey found, in order:

- ○ **Search engines**
- ○ **USENET Newsgroups**
- ○ **cool lists - these are lists of sites deemed to be worth visiting compiled by search engines or independent parties**
- ○ **new lists**
- ○ **listservers**
- ○ **print ads**
- ○ **word of mouth and e-mail signature files**
- ○ **topical indexes**
- ○ **linked Webvertissements**
- ○ **random links from content pages**
- ○ **jump sites - these are listings sites. For example, the Charities Aid Foundation < http://www.charitynet.org > has a jump site listing UK charities and charity resources. They are there to take users to sites relating to a specific subject**

Publicising your pages: the Internet

Linking your pages to other related pages

Use a search engine to find related sites (for example, your suppliers or stakeholders) and post a polite e-mail to the Webmaster of that site requesting a link to your site. It is polite to reciprocate by creating a link from your site to theirs.

Linking your pages to search engines

Register the site with the appropriate search engines, both directories and indexes. Some of the most popular ones include:

www.altavista.digital.com	www.eiNet.Net	www.god.co.uk
www.excite.com	www.infoseek.com	www.inktomi.com
www.lycos.com	www.opentext.com	www.yell.co.uk
www.Webcrawler.com	www.yahoo.com	www.search.com

Beaucoup <http://www.beaucoup.com> has links to over 400 search engines listed by 14 categories from around the world.

A good one-stop shop for submitting your pages to some of the most popular search engines is Submit It <http://www.submit-it.com>

You can pay a company to index your site. On some search engines you can include keywords to be indexed and a description of your site.

When embarking upon a session to register your site have ready:

- ○ **the title of your Web site**
- ○ **the address of your Web site**
- ○ **the contact person and details for the site**
- ○ **a list of keywords for your site**
- ○ **a short description of your Web site**

Some search engines take over six weeks to list your site once you have submitted it. You can check to see which search engines have your site listed with did-it <http://www.did-it.com/>.

Win an award

Winning an award such as Cool Site of the Day will certainly get your site known about. Award-It! <http://www.award-it.com>, is a one-stop registration form to apply to several award sites.

E-Zines

On-line magazines often include links to or reviews of Web sites, so it is worth sending them details of your pages. A list of E-zines can be found at <http://www.dominis.com/Zines/>

In Newsgroups

Newsgroups are a good way of spreading the word about your Web site. It is not, however, a good idea simply to post details of your Web site in relevant Newsgroups, this is likely to incite bad feeling towards your organisation and may even result in you being flamed - or rebuked on-line.

The way to publicise your Web site is to *lurk* in appropriate Newsgroups and, when relevant, mention your Web site in response to a posting.

Most Newsgroups will have an associated FAQ (list of Frequently Asked Questions) which will explain what is and is not acceptable behaviour in that particular Newsgroup in regard to publicising Web sites.

Several Newsgroups exist specifically to announce new Web sites:
comp.infosystems.www.announce
uk.events
uk.misc

E-mail signature files

E-mail signature files are small text files which are added to the bottom of your e-mails. Include details of your organisation's site in the e-mail signature file of all employees.

Publicising your pages: traditional media

National press

The following newspapers all have Internet sections which carry news about what is new on the Web and it is worth sending them a copy of your press release with a note requesting a mention.

The Independent Network - David Bowen Network@independent.co.uk
The Scotsman - david.calder@almac.co.uk/100432,3654@compuserve.com
The Times Interface - times.Interface@dial.pipex.com
The Guardian On-line - on-line@guardian.co.uk

Net magazines

Internet - paulb@Internet.emap.com
Internet World - Gus Venditto venditto@iw.com
.Net - Cotton Ward cward@futureNet.co.uk
New Scientist Netropolitan - edit@news.newsci.ipc.co.uk

It is also worth checking to see if there are any magazines, newsletters or trade press related to your activities that have a Web presence with a column announcing new Web sites. News of Internet activity is becoming a regular feature of many trade journals.

Publicising your Web pages elsewhere

Feature the site address prominently on all paper-based organisational literature such as letterhead, business cards, leaflets and brochures, annual reports and advertisements. Also you could add your Web address to your franking machine stamp. Include a copy of the press release in any mailout. It is also worth sending a copy of the press release to a list of key contacts, either by e-mail or by snail mail.

Think about events at which the site could be promoted. A computer terminal with the site's files stored locally and a Web browser are all that are needed to provide facilities for people to browse your site without actually being connected to the Internet. Possible events could include an annual general meeting, conferences, trade shows.

It may also be worth announcing your Web site at a special launch event - perhaps held at a local Cybercafe with an Internet guru as guest speaker.

Do not forget that many of the above techniques will pull in first time visitors. It is then up to you to convert those into repeat visits.

Summary

O   The Web is the most common part of the Internet used for marketing.

O   There are four main stages in developing a marketing Web site: building content; building the web site; putting the site onto the Internet and marketing your Web site.

O   One of the most important features of your Web site is the navigation - a well designed Web site will use good, clear navigation to move prospects through the marketing cycle.

O   The three main ways of attracting traffic to your Web site are to engage users, provide customised content and offer value added content.

O   Choosing a Web designer with the   right skills and appropriate marketing experience is key to the marketing success of your Web site.

O   It is your job to let people know how to find your Web site, by marketing it on the Internet through search engines and through traditional communication channels.

8 Marketing by E-mail and Newsgroups

Marketing via e-mail

More people have e-mail access than Web access. Used appropriately, e-mail can be effective for marketing your product or service.

It is possible to purchase e-mail mailing lists from direct mail list brokers but these may not always be reliable because of the methods they use to assemble the addresses. Beware of organisations selling you bulk e-mailing facilities - these are collections of short adverts from hundreds of different advertisers which are sent in one e-mail message and are not a very effective way of marketing via e-mail.

The best method of marketing via e-mail is to use e-mail addresses that have been collected from a Listserv mailing list. Mailing lists are discussions conducted entirely via e-mail. Users ask to subscribe to a mailing list on a specific subject and then receive (by e-mail) any e-mail messages forwarded to that list. Users choose to receive e-mails on a particular topic. E-mail lists that have been compiled from Listserv mailing lists can provide your organisation with direct contact to a very targeted audience.

Unsolicited e-mail, or junk-e-mail, is severely frowned upon. Remember that marketing by e-mail is unlike other forms of direct mail in that the recipient in most cases has to pay to receive your message. By indiscriminately e-mailing to a broad unresearched audience you will create resentment towards your organisation, even if the recipient of your e-mail message might be interested in your product or service. Many users will bin unsolicited e-mail on sight. Others will send your e-mail to a kill file which prevents your e-mails ever reaching that person again. Worse, you may get a mention on the blacklist of Internet advertisers and the whole world will get to hear of your bad practices.

The Direct Electronic Mail Marketing Association <http://www.memo. net/demma/dema.html> is a professional association dedicated to providing education and technical assistance to consumers and businesses that send and receive commercial e-mail via the Internet. They seek to foster goodwill among the consumers of the Internet by providing the means for subscribing to commercial mailing lists and reducing the amount of unsolicited commercial e-mail on the net.

E-mail signature files

These are a simple but effective marketing tool. Trail some current offer briefly in the signature file of your e-mail, then add a link direct to your site, give details of current special offers - with a link to that section on your site. Change them often.

E-mail newsletters

Short e-mail newsletters with helpful articles can be an effective way of keeping in touch with prospective customers, reminding them of your existence and services.

Marketing via Newsgroups

Fewer Internet users have access to Newsgroups - perhaps only half. Newsgroups can be used to create a community around your product or service.

It is a good idea to subscribe to, and participate in, Newsgroups that reach your target market, so if you are selling health-related products, visit the health-related Newsgroups. Become an active participant of a Newsgroup.

If a person comments that they are looking for a solution to accomplish a particular task and your product or service meets this need there is nothing wrong with mentioning your solution - you must also mention that you work for the company. It is also a good idea to set up a Newsgroup community of people interested in your products. Company employees can share experiences and information with users of the group. This will help to build customer loyalty as well as being an excellent way of providing customer support.

Using Newsgroups to advertise your products or services should be approached with care. Inappropriate advertising involves sending messages to unrelated Newsgroups or to those which traditionally do not tolerate commercial messages. In general, advertising is not permitted in Newsgroups. Read the Frequently Asked Questions (FAQ) for a Newsgroup and check carefully whether commercial advertising is permitted and how to go about it.

The biz.* and *.marketplace Newsgroups are the places to go to advertise products and services but even there you must do your research and abide by the rules of a particular Newsgroup.

Spamming

Spamming refers to the practice of posting multiple copies of the same message to many Newsgroups. Such practices are considered bad Netiquette amongst the Internet community and can result, in the worst cases, in your Internet access being pulled.

If people receive spam they will filter your e-mail and/or spread negative word-of-mouth about your advertising practices. It is not worth the risk.

Netiquette

Netiquette is the collection of informal rules which govern behaviour on the Internet and business use of the Internet. They are taken very seriously and the penalties for breaching them can be severe.

Canter and Siegel, two immigration lawyers, made Internet history with their spectacular breach of Newsgroup advertising netiquette, and were widely reprimanded and shunned by the Internet community. In 1994, they repeatedly sent out a message offering their services in helping to enter the US greencard lottery to almost all usenet Newsgroups. Their mail server was mail bombed (sent large crippling e-mails which brought the system to a halt) and their Internet Service Provider stopped their access.

When using mass communication tools such as e-mail and Newsgroups for marketing purposes it pays to respect the culture and communities that use these tools.

Do's and don'ts of marketing via e-mail and Newsgroups

- *don't post adverts to Newsgroups unless explicitly allowed*
- *don't cross-post to several Newsgroups*
- *don't send unsolicited e-mail*
- *do take the time to familiarise yourself with the culture of a particular Newsgroup before making a contribution of any sort.*

Summary

○   Although e-mail is perhaps the most widely used tool on the Internet, its uses for marketing are limited by acceptable behaviour on the Internet.

○   Marketing in Newsgroups is also restricted by netiquette, including the practice of posting multiple copies of the same message to several Newsgroups.

9 New Technologies and their Impact on Marketing on the Internet

The best Internet marketing strategies integrate many different media and technologies. However, the goalposts seem to be shifting daily as new technologies appear. Marketers need to keep abreast of the latest emerging Internet technologies and understand how they work and can be integrated to meet consumer needs. There are two main issues to take into consideration when looking at the impact of the latest technologies when marketing on the Internet:

O *Is the technology currently available to your target audience?* Many Browsers do not support all the latest technologies or else they require the user to download plug-ins in order to view them. In addition, your target audience may not have the necessary bandwidth to comfortably access the latest technologies - which often require large files that take a long time to download. Marketers must be able to translate consumers' needs into the right mix of interactivity and multimedia while at the same time bearing in mind the current limitations of the Internet - such as bandwidth restrictions and Browser support. Adopting new technologies that are not widely supported can create a negative experience for your audience.

O *Does the technology solve specific marketing problems?* The key here is to focus on the solution offered to marketing problems and not the technology itself.

Active Content

As the Web advances into the next century the balance of focus will shift heavily towards Web sites using the latest technologies to deliver rich content. These technologies will be quickly integrated and consumers will demand more value and functionality from Web sites.

Here are some of the emerging new technologies that are impacting on the Internet:

Interactivity Programming and scripting languages such as Java, Javascript and ActiveX are enabling new ways of interacting over the Web.

Java truly brings the Web alive. Java is an object-oriented programming language, similar to C++, developed by Sun Microsystems. It makes the Web truly interactive. For instance, a Web page could include an image which can be clicked on by the browser and rotated in any direction. Or a Web page could be linked to a real time data feed such as livestock prices with these being scrolled across the page. Java can be used to create chat rooms in your Web site which can be used for market research purposes or simply to attract traffic to your site. It can also be used to create animations on your page. Java is behind calculators used for mortgages, insurance and currency exchange.

Interactive games and puzzles can provide both entertainment and education - these can be programmed in Java. They are popular on the Web and will help to attract traffic to your site. Small Java applications (or applets as they are known) which enable this interactivity can be called from a Web page. Javascript is a scripting language which enables animations and scrolling information.

Microsoft has brought out its own technology for creating active content in Web sites called ActiveX. ActiveX uses controls which are little programs that add functionality to Web pages.

Dynamic HTML is a new HTML standard which is being pushed by both Microsoft and Netscape in differing formats to allow greater flexibility and interaction with Web pages - such as users being able to move elements around a Web page - without using bandwidth-consuming technologies that require plug-ins.

Another method of interacting with your audience is to use real-time Web-chat areas on your Web pages. These have been around for a while but are just starting to be applied for marketing purposes.

Web-chat is real-time chat over a Web page. You type something, it then appears on the Web page for people to respond to. Web-chat can include video and multimedia so you can see the people you are chatting to and include graphics in your conversation.

One marketing use of Web-chat may be to have a customer services representative, support staff or even a professional adviser offering their services as a taster on-line to encourage full purchase of these services.

In marketing terms the new more interactive technologies will help marketers with:

○   **Relationship marketing: improving dialogue with stakeholders**
○   **Personalised marketing: providing consumer-selected content which specifically meets their needs**
○   **Improving response rate and customer service**

National Semiconductor *<http://www.natsemi.com>* *put its entire product line on the Web and uses a search engine written in Java to provide high-speed, interactive searching. The system enables design engineers and other users to search National Semiconductor's product database and to select attributes of interest without having to know any part-numbering sequence, datasheet naming scheme or description text. Users can select component attributes such as power levels, tolerances and package types, successively narrowing the list of suitable products until a subset of appropriate products is identified. Designers can then select from a variety of product information on those products, including data sheets, pricing and availability, performance ranges and, eventually, characterization data generated by National's lab.*

This kind of application represents the way that business will provide product information to their users in the future.

Databases on the Web   Live databases, where users can access up-to-date information in real time on the Web, and generally improved database connectivity will provide a strategic advantage to companies as well as marketing benefits, such as improved customer service and reduced administrative costs.

3D environments VRML (Virtual Reality Markup Language) enables virtual reality 3D environments to be visualised on the Web allowing you to interact with objects in those environments and link to other objects and Web pages. The Energy Savings Trust <http://www.est.org.uk> uses a 3D house to educate users on energy savings. The users navigate around the house, clicking on objects which reveal pop-up menus detailing cost-savings and energy-saving materials. Future applications of 3D technologies could be in creating new shopping environments on the Web.

Audio Real-time audio (also known as streamed audio - because audio is sent in a continuous uninterrupted stream in real-time) is now possible in a Web site, although not widely used or popular because it consumes a lot of Internet bandwidth. The most popular streamed audio product is RealAudio from Progressive Networks <http://www.realaudio.com>.

Video Video on the Web is also possible using software such as RealVideo from the people who brought RealAudio, QuickTime VR, VDOLive and MPEG. However, real-time video is also limited by available bandwidth.

The obvious marketing use of streamed audio and video is for product sampling, for instance of music CDs.

Push

Push, or Web broadcasting as it is also known, is the new face of the Web and is a very effective way for marketers to target specific groups. Instead of users actively seeking and pulling information and pages from the Web, content is delivered to the user according to a set of defined criteria to view off-line. For example, users may select to receive only business-related information on the Web. Software such as PointCast and Castanet delivers information to the desktop via a screensaver or scrolling window.

PointCast <http://www.pointcast.com> consists of a channel viewer on your desktop and the PointCast Network which is a series of Servers located in the US which holds the content provided by 45 media companies such as Reuters and CNN. Users select channels from which they wish to receive information.

Content at the moment is US-centric. You can keep up to date on weather, news, company share prices, your personal horoscope. PointCast is available free of charge.

Castanet <http://www.marimba.com> is very similar to PointCast. It uses a tuner and you can then subscribe to any number of channels. After you install and run Castanet you first need to choose a Transmitter. Then you choose the channels from that Transmitter you would like to receive information from, and how often you would like to receive updates. As well as information Castanet also delivers applications which are automatically updated.

A more European-specific content provider which delivers content via Push was launched in the second quarter of 1997. Lanacom's Headliner <http://www.lanacom.com> has more than 400 channels from which to choose. The Electronic Telegraph and BBC have channels on the service. Content can be delivered via a small scrolling news bar or across the title bar of an active application or screensaver. Warnings that a page has changed can also be sent to your screen.

Organisations can also use Push technology to deliver directly from their own Web sites without going through one-stop channelling services such as PointCast.

Push technology is also used to deliver up-to-date information to employees' desktops via corporate Intranets. INCISCA is aimed at the Intranet market.

Companies will be able to use Push technology to target marketing messages to specifically interested consumers. If someone subscribes to, or uses, a Push channel that monitors xyz then marketers can be pretty confident that they are interested in xyz. From then on advertising messages related to xyz can be targeted directly to the interested user.

Technologies such as Push are bringing highly targeted micro marketing one step closer.

Intranets

Whilst Intranets have been around now for a few years and over 60% of large companies already have one, they are only just being used as strategic business tools.

Intranets are internal Internets which use the same protocols, standards and tools as the public Internet but they are private within organisations. They enable users of Local Area Networks to publish and access information using the familiar and easy-to-use World Wide Web front end to send and receive internal e-mail.

Intranets can be used to improve communications between employees in sales, marketing and product development as well as offering increased accessibility to product and sales information, catalogued, indexed and searchable. This provides clear advantages for marketing professionals both in terms of reduced costs - savings on printing and distribution of product sales catalogues to employees, and in terms of efficiency - consider the effect of a fully informed and up-to-date sales force.

Extranets

Extranets are business-to-business private networks which use Internet protocols. They are being used by businesses to provide vital information on products and services direct to their client base; many use them for product ordering and selling via catalogues.

Wiznet in the US <http://www.uscommerce.com/index70.html> offers PurchasingExtranet, the largest collection of industrial and manufacturing products and services catalogues in the world with secure direct communication between buyers and sellers. Products can be located in their database according to a number of criteria including form, fit or function, supplier or trade agreement and part number.

Network computers

Network Computers - known as NCs are inexpensive set-top boxes that can be plugged into a TV or monitor and provide access to the Internet. The NetStation <http://www.netproducts.net> is one of the first such products aimed at the consumer market. It combines TV, Web and e-mail and can be connected to VCRs and printers. Access to the Net is provided by NetChannel which calls itself the first television service provider (TVSP). Market Research company Forrester Research predicts that 14.7 million households with TVs could be connected to the Internet by 2002. The arrival of these cheap and easy-to-use net access TVs throws a challenge to marketers to develop appropriate consumer-orientated Web sites. They also open up channels for Internet shopping.

Internet telephony

Internet telephony means that Web sites can be integrated with the telephone system. By clicking a button you can be put through to someone over the Net. On your Web site you could offer a direct link, for example, with a customer services representative.

NetCall in the UK offers Web call-back: this is a link from a Web site to a page where users input their phone number and instantly receive a call-back over a standard line. This is cheaper than using 0800 numbers.

Answer Communications <http://www.realcall.com> is offering a call-back solution called RealCall. They provide a button which is embedded in a Web page. When the button is clicked, a message comes up notifying the user that a customer services representative will call. Messages can be customised to say 'call me in five minutes'. The customer does not pay for the call; this is billed to the site owner.

Secure electronic transactions

The secure electronic transactions specification SET will provide a secure way to process credit card payment transactions over the Internet. This will facilitate the growth of on-line shopping. See Chapter 6 on Selling over the Internet for further details on the progress of secure electronic transactions technologies.

Summary

O   **New technologies are enabling enhanced interactivity and therefore offer the opportunity to improve dialogue with stakeholders.**

O   Micro-marketing is also being given a boost with Push
    applications.

O   When implementing new technologies into your Internet
    marketing strategy you must be careful not to exclude users
    who may not be able to view them.

O   Internet protocols are being used to extend the utilities of
    the Internet into the organisation via Intranets and between
    organisations via Extranets.

O   New mass consumer products such as TV set top boxes
    and NCs could make home on-line shopping more
    accessible.

10 Monitoring Results and Evolving Strategy

Assessing and improving the effectiveness of your Internet marketing strategy involves:

○ **Choosing and putting into place the necessary monitoring tools and mechanisms**
○ **Interpreting the results**
○ **Adjusting your strategy in the light of these results**

One of your first tasks when setting up your Internet marketing strategy is to set a clear set of aims and objectives. From these you then derive quantifiable targets, such as 'to increase monthly sales by x'. Some targets may not be as easily or directly quantifiable, such as 'to raise the organisation's profile'. It is important then, to define a time-frame in which to achieve these targets and then set up a review process, at specific intervals - say, every 3 months - to evaluate whether you are on track and whether there are any adjustments to be made to bring the targets closer. You may even decide to move the goalposts, based on data and information that you have gleaned from your evaluation process. There are various methods for monitoring effectiveness of Internet strategy. They can be divided into quantitative and qualitative measurement tools.

Quantitative measurement

Quantitative measurements can include:

○ **the number of hits to your Web site**

- the number of e-mails you receive, either generally to the company or to particular departments
- the number of times your organisation, product or service is mentioned in Newsgroups
- the number of completed forms received from your Web site
- the number of sales generated directly from your Web site

Logfile analysis

The first step in monitoring the effectiveness of your Web marketing strategy is usually to compile and analyse statistics of who is accessing your Web site, what pages are being accessed most frequently, and when.

Your Internet Service Provider, or whoever hosts your Web site, keeps a logfile of access statistics for your Web pages, stored on the Web server. If you are renting server space from a Service Provider, usage statistics will be formatted and either be made accessible to you via the Web as a Web page (and therefore public) or e-mailed to you as a private service regularly by your Service Provider.

Interpreting logfiles

Logfiles in their raw state are lines of code and, whilst simple enough to interpret, can be rather daunting when the files are large. If you are running your own Web server there are many tools available to automate the analysis. Two of the best are Webtrends <http://www.webtrends.com> and Hit List Pro <http://www.marketwave.com>.

The number of hits for each page or graphic

Using the number of hits to your site alone as a measurement of its success is a very dubious method. Hits refer not to the number of users but to the number of files - HTML or graphic, for example - that the Web server has served or attempted to serve. So, a single user may have requested one page which contains many files and each of these will count as a separate hit.

Other hindrances to recording hits accurately are caching systems. When you access a Web page the files that make up that Web page are downloaded into a special storage area on your hard drive called a cache. The next time you access those pages they will be read from the cache and not from the remote Web server. Your second reading therefore, will not count as a hit.

In addition, some countries and organisations use proxy servers which store identical copies of a Web site locally. When a user requests a page from that Web site they are retrieved from the local server and not from the host Web server. Thousands of users may access your Web site from a proxy server but none of these will register as a hit.

Logfiles can help you rethink the navigation and accessibility of your Web site. It may be that people are not accessing a particular page because it is buried in your Web site and not easy to find.

They can also help you to improve your pages - by recording which pages are being accessed and how often, you can tell which pages are most popular and which are not. You can then use that information to improve your pages by changing either the content, layout, design or functionality.

Logfiles can be used to determine whether people are accessing your pages with image-loading facilities turned off - by counting the number of HTML files that are downloaded without corresponding image files. Keep a lookout for users who download the first page of your site with images and then switch image loading off. Does your site have too many images? Are the images badly designed and unclear? Are your users low bandwidth users?

The same is true of multimedia files.

Domain name

Domain names of those accessing your pages are sometimes expressed as an IP address (a numeric address that uniquely identifies a computer on the Internet), including the number of hits per domain.

Whilst this data will give you an indication of which domains are accessing your site most often, beware of interpreting domain names as users from a particular type of organisation or country. For example, a UK company may well have the international domain name .com in its address. An ISP's domain name may be hiding either an individual or an organisation.

Hits that originate from organisations with firewalls are deceptive. There may be thousands of people from an organisation accessing your site but showing up as only one person.

Users with dial-up access may also be difficult to pinpoint - they are not always assigned the same IP address twice.

Where people are coming from can give you a good idea as to how effective you have been at promoting your site and which search engines or Web sites are generating the most traffic to it.

Date, time and duration of access

This information is useful in determining how long users remain on your site and on particular pages. This may help you in deciding which are the most popular pages and which pages need improving. It may also be that your Web site is popular at certain particular times - if, for example, you offer a local events guide you may find traffic increasing at weekends and will need to make adequate hardware and access provision for this.

Check your link strategy. If users are leaving your site at the first page to follow the links to other sites you have provided, you may want to rethink your linking strategy and, in particular, the placement of links.

One word of warning - time spent on a page is not always a precise measurement of involvement - it will not tell you, for instance, whether the user got up to make a cup of tea whilst seemingly accessing your page.

The browser that the client is using

Logfiles are useful in helping you to decide what features to add to your site. For example, should you be using Netscape Navigator or Internet Explorer specific features? If the majority of accesses to your Web site are made using the latest version of Netscape you can be confident that if you use Netscape extensions to HTML, your users will be able to view them comfortably.

The results of requests for files

This will tell you whether a Web page was successfully retrieved and returned to the browser or not. You may be familiar with the message 'error - 404 not found' coming up in your Browser after you have typed in an address or clicked on a link. This could be because the user has typed the incorrect address, or the file has been moved or renamed. Similarly, noted in the logfiles are indications where the server has failed to fulfil an apparently valid request. This can reveal the reliability of your Web server and the suitability of the connection to it, and whether the links in your site are correct and up-to-date.

Translating logfile interpretations into evolving your strategy

Analysing logfiles can be a revealing exercise the deeper you go. The number of times people access your home page may not tell you much. But the number of people who visited your product information, and how long they stayed there and whether they made a purchase at the end of it and if they returned, can give you a good idea of the effectiveness of your Internet marketing efforts.

Think also about your Web promotion strategy. It may be that if you are getting a low hit count, it is because few people know that you have a site or where to find it. See Chapter 8 for details on promoting your Web site.

Sales figures

Sales figures are, perhaps, one of the most common methods of evaluating the effectiveness of an Internet marketing strategy because they provide a direct indication of your stakeholders' reactions to your on-line marketing efforts. They are also readily available. It is a simple process to quantify sales made directly over the Internet. It is less easy, however, to gauge sales that have been made indirectly as a result of your Internet marketing strategy. For example, someone may telephone their order in as a result of seeing your Web site or of receiving a direct marketing e-mail from you or seeing your product or organisation mentioned in a Newsgroup.

When using sales figures as a measure of the success of your Web site make sure that you are counting sales that you would not have made otherwise and not merely sales displaced from traditional channels. You will need qualitative information, perhaps from a survey, in order to fully evaluate the percentage of new sales from the Internet compared with those that have been transferred from other channels.

A survey for the Wall Street Journal discovered that whilst 29 per cent of UK companies had increased sales over the Internet, only half that number had actually made a profit from it.

Measuring success with advertising on the Internet

Perhaps one of the areas of the Internet that has advanced furthest in terms of developing methods of measuring success is advertising. This is partly because traditional methods of measurement are adaptable to the Internet and because of the rigorous demands for quantifiable measurements required to draw advertisers on to it.

One quantitative measurement criterion being used is the number of impressions per advert. Impressions are the number of times the Web advertisement has been shown to the user.

Click through rate - the number of times a user clicks on the advert and goes through to the client's site - is also being used to measure an advert's success. Logfile statistics can tell you where a user has come from. This gives you valuable information about which advertising slots generate the most hits. Using sales as a measurement of advertising success is as problematic on-line as it is in other media. It is not so easy to measure precisely the success of advertising on the Internet in terms of sales because there are so many factors that affect sales quite independently of advertising.

Traditional methods, such as recall and recognition tests, can be used to evaluate Web advertisements - as can focus groups and on-line surveys.

These can be useful for measuring changes in attitude, and brand awareness as a result of the advert's presence on a Web site. The Audit Bureau of Circulations (ABC) and the Business Publications Association (BPA) both offer Web auditing services for the UK which verify the claims made by sites with regard to their apparent success.

Qualitative measurement

Whilst quantitative statistics are helpful in determining which are the most popular pages on your site - whether you are reaching the right audience and whether your data is presented in a way acceptable to users - it is not the final measure of success. In order to assess the site fully you cannot rely on quantitative data alone. Further qualitative data must be gathered - for example, using simple feedback questionnaires on the site which ask specific questions.

Good quality feedback from your site is a sure sign of a successful marketing strategy.

Here are some questions you might ask:

O   **how useful and accessible is the Web site?**
O   **how do customers rate your organisation as a result of your Internet marketing activities?**
O   **how do customers rate your products and services as a result of your Internet marketing activities?**
O   **have consumers bought your product or service as a result of your Internet marketing campaign, when they might not have done so otherwise?**
O   **what are the evolving needs of customers visiting your Web site?**

However, response rates for voluntary questionnaires are sometimes very low and a much more focused and organised approach to obtaining feedback is required. This could be in the form of usability groups, or focus groups.

Evolving your strategy

The feedback, both qualitative and quantitative, generated from your Web site should be fed into the development process of your site.

The key is to convert missed opportunities into direct response. Many of the main variables of a Web site, layout, design, language, etc. can be modified, sometimes only slightly, to provoke the required response. Feedback from monitoring should help you to pinpoint which variables may need tweaking. It is then up to you to evolve your strategy to reflect these changes.

The marketing environment

The Internet marketing environment is one that is driven by new technological changes and characterised by uncertainty. To capitalise on opportunities and cope with adversity, marketers will need to monitor the marketing environment and adapt accordingly. Adapting may involve building new functionality into your Web site - for instance, as security issues are resolved and offer secure credit card payment options. It may involve re-thinking and re-organising your traditional marketing methods or even doing away with them completely as the focus of a new marketing environment in the Internet era changes and evolves.

It will also be a marketing advantage to your organisation to adopt new technologies ahead of the game.

A dynamic environment

The fantasy that a Web site is ever finished is just that. Many sites put up 'work in progress' signs on their Web sites, but with a Web site it is always in progress. The key to a successful marketing Web site is establishing a dialogue with stakeholders which involves constantly updated material. Users will not return to your site if it remains static. By offering regularly updated content you will give people a reason to come back to your site and convert visits into an ongoing dialogue.

Unlike other media, once the original content is created, the incremental cost of adding more pages is almost zero.

It is important to let users know when they can expect information to be updated,or they will soon tire of checking your site to see if there is anything new. Marketing Week <http://www.marketing-week.co.uk/mw0001/>, for example, lets its readers know that at one minute past midnight their site will be updated and the 00:01 theme runs throughout the site.

More than simply telling them when your site will be updated, give them a reason to return by telling them what they will get if they do.

Even better, offer a reminder service to users, where they give you their e-mail address and you notify them by e-mail of any changes to the site. The Pure Fiction <http://www.purefiction.com> site offers this service. Whenever the content of the site changes, users are notified by e-mail that changes have occurred and what these are. There are also update services available such as URL Minder <http://www.netmind.com/URL-minder/URL-minder.html> that will inform users when changes to your site occur. These kinds of reminder service are especially useful if your content is updated infrequently.

It is not enough to draw up a strategy for evolving your content. You must ensure that the necessary resources are actually made available and allocate responsibility for maintaining and updating your Web site - through a maintenance contract with an Internet services company, or work in-house.

A fluid and dynamic marketing site is one that becomes streamlined and easier to navigate over time, with clearly customer-driven content. LOOT <http://www.loot.co.uk>, the classified advertisements Web site, has changed 5 times since its inception in response to feedback from users and advertisers. The design has become simpler with no frames, fewer graphics and simple colours.

Beware the danger of simply adding pages onto your Web site willy nilly - make sure that new pages are incorporated into the overall structure and design. Don't be afraid to revise your original structure and design if need be - this is better than an out-of-control structure resulting from adding pages on thoughtlessly.

There are site management tools available which make the job of maintaining links and spotting missing files easier. Astra Site Manager <http://www.merc-int.com/products/astrasmguide.html>, Linkbot <http:// www.tetranetsoftware. com/linkbot-info.htm> and Adobe SiteMill <http:// www.adobe.co.uk/ products/pagemill/pagemill.html> are examples of some of the better ones.

These can then be used with an HTML editor to fix any problems.

A successful Internet marketing strategy

Your Internet marketing strategy should not be stagnant. Your strategy should follow a cycle of developing marketing objectives and targets, implementing marketing strategy, evaluating performance relative to objectives and targets and taking corrective action and, thus, constantly evolving your Internet marketing strategy.

The rewards are plenty. A fully integrated, well thought out and implemented Internet marketing strategy can translate into new sales, good publicity for your organisation, enhanced profile and awareness of your products and services, a loyal clientele and a motivated and efficient marketing team.

Summary

- Both quantitative and qualitative tools should be used when measuring the success of your Internet marketing strategy.
- The number of hits on your Web site is not a reliable measure of the success of your Internet marketing campaign and such figures must be interpreted cautiously.
- A more traditional way of measuring the success of your Internet marketing strategy is to count the number of new sales it has generated.
- The results of your qualitative and quantitative measurements should be used to develop and evolve your Internet marketing strategy.
- A successful Internet marketing strategy is one that is responsive and adaptable to environmental changes.
- Web sites are dynamic and should be regularly updated to maintain your audience's interest.

Glossary

Acrobat Adobe's software package for storing and displaying electronic documents so that they retain their formatting, no matter to which computer platform they are transferred. Acrobat is now a standard method of storing and viewing certain documents on the Internet.

Advertorials These are Web sites which have strong branding and related editorial content.

Auto-responder Also known as a mailbot or autobot, this is a software package that enables a standard message or file to be sent back in response to an e-mail message. Auto-responders are very useful for reducing the workload of sending out standard messages and forms.

Bandwidth The amount of data that can be transmitted over a communication channel.

Banner adverts Single 480x60 pixel graphics, either animated or static, that appear on Web pages. They are used for advertising and usually link to the advertiser's Web site.

Boolean search A method of searching for information, in particular words or phrases, using the logical operators AND, OR and NOT.

Browser A software program used for reading hypertext eg World Wide Web pages. Common browsers include Netscape Navigator and Microsoft Internet Explorer.

Common Gateway Interface (CGI) A standard method of integrating software packages such as databases and spreadsheets with World Wide Web pages. CGI scripts are written in a computer programming language, usually Perl.

Cookies Small data files downloaded with Web sites that sit on the computer's hard drive recording information about the user and their activities on the Web.

CPM (Cost per thousand impressions) The unit used to cost advertising space on Web sites.

Disintermediation Refers to the electronic integration of supply chains resulting from producers cutting out the middlemen and dealing directly with consumers over the Internet.

Domain name system (DNS) System for converting the numeric Internet addresses of computers and systems into more easily-recognisable domain names and vice versa eg. 123.456.78.9 becomes myname.mycomputer.org.uk

Download To copy or move a file from a computer on the Internet or a computer network to your computer.

E-mail Electronic mail is a method of sending text messages and other computer files from one computer to another (or many other) computers via the Internet or a computer network.

Encryption Encoding or otherwise concealing text or files to prevent others from accessing them, often useful when sending sensitive data such as credit card details over the Internet.

Enmeshing Linking pages *within* your own Web site.

Extranet Two or more Intranets connected together.

FAQ A list of answers to Frequently Asked Questions posted to e-mail discussion lists Web sites or Usenet Newsgroups.

Flame An angry, often abusive e-mail message, criticising or objecting to a message or comment you have sent eg. to a Newsgroup or e-mail discussion list. An exchange of flames, an online argument, is a flamewar. It usually achieves nothing except wasting other subscribers' time.

Forms Text areas on a Web page into which users can input data direct and this returned to the Server for processing.

Freeware (public domain) Software which is given away at no charge to users. Many freeware software packages are available on the Internet. Freeware should not be confused with shareware.

FTP File Transfer Protocol, a standard method of transferring a computer file from one computer to another via the Internet.

Gateway A computer or computer system which acts as a bridge or link between two different computer networks, thereby enabling the exchange of files between them.

GIF Graphics Interchange Format, a standard type of graphics file format used in incorporating images on World Wide Web pages. GIFs have the file suffix .GIF, for example, image.gif

Hit The viewing of a World Wide Web page i.e. the accessing of the page's HTML file. Each hit is recorded automatically by the computer system on which the page is stored. Records of such hits on different pages can be interpreted to determine the number or type of visitors to a World Wide Web site. However, ten hits on a page could mean ten visitors to that page or, equally, it could mean one visitor accessing the page ten times.

Home page The default World Wide Web page that is loaded when the browser is first started. It could be a personal page, a charity's main page, or the browser manufacturer's main page.

HTML HyperText Mark-up Language is the standard Internet code in which World Wide Web pages are written. Text, graphics, sounds, video and other devices are all presented using a series of text tags, eg. <P> signifies a paragraph break. The resultant text files are interpreted and displayed by World Wide Web browser software programs. HTML ensures that the type of computer on which the file is stored and the type of computer on which the file is viewed is effectively irrelevant.

HTML offers the flexibility of storing and presenting information in hypertext.

HTTP Hypertext Transfer Protocol is a standard method of transferring HTML documents over the Internet.

Hypertext A method of linking information on one computer file to associated information on another. This is the method of storing and structuring information that underpins the World Wide Web.

Intelligent Agents An Intelligent Agent is a piece of software that you can 'train' or give a set of instructions to, such as finding information on a certain topic for you on the Web, and it will go away and do it.

Internet Explorer The World Wide Web browser provided by Microsoft, originally as part of its Windows 95 software.

Internet Service Provider (ISP) An ISP (more accurately an IAP - Internet Access Provider) is a company which provides public access to their Internet-connected LAN or WAN. This is analogous to a telephone exchange, where public access points into the global voice network are provided.

Interstitials Interstitials are 5 to 10 second animated ads which appear without having to click on anything. They take up the whole of the screen and are played before receiving the content of the Web site they are hosted on.

Intranet An internal computer network within an organisation which uses Internet tools and programs for private use and restricted access only. The Intranet might allow access to the Internet to the organisation's staff but it will not allow access to unauthorised users outside the system.

ISDN Integrated Service Digital Network provides much faster and more secure transmission of voice and computer files than that which is available over a standard telephone line.

JAVA A programming language.

JPEG Joint Photographic Experts Group who produced the JPEG standard graphics file format which, like GIF, is commonly used on World Wide Web pages.

Local area network (LAN) Local Area Network, a computer network usually within one organisation, which enables people to share data, eg. via e-mail, and hardware such as printers. A LAN can be connected to another LAN or to the Internet with a gateway. One or more computers acts as a server where documents, printers, etc. are located. The connections are often Ethernet using cheap coaxial or twisted-pair cable, and limited in length. Bandwidth is usually 10Mbps.

Logfiles Logfiles sit on your Web server and record who is visiting your site, how they arrived there, which country they are from, how long they stay, which is the most popular content accessed and when.

Leased line/dedicated line A private telephone line that is permanently connected to the Internet. This is the opposite to a dial-up link which uses the line only for the duration of the telephone call.

Listserv Software that runs an e-mail discussion list automatically. It is sometimes used generically of all e-mail discussion lists, irrespective of the software used to run them, eg. Majordomo, Listproc.

Mailing list/e-mail list A system, usually automated, that distributes e-mail messages on a specific topic to the e-mailboxes of a list of subscribers. Some lists are one-way, allowing a charity, for example, to send out regular announcements. Others are two-way and allow messages to be posted by any subscriber, thereby allowing an ongoing conversation between two or more subscribers that is viewed by all subscribers. Subscription is usually free and requires an e-mail message to be sent to the central list software program.

Micropayments Low-cost small payment transactions over the Internet.

Modem Device that converts digital data such as computer files and messages so that it can be sent across the non-digital telephone network to another computer. Similarly, it reconverts such data back into digital form which can be received and processed by a computer.

Multimedia Video, sound, graphics and animation.

Net An abbreviation for the Internet.

Netiquette A largely unwritten set of rules of behaviour on the Internet, widely adhered to - mostly because they are common sense and make life easier.

Netscape Navigator The most popular World Wide Web browser used on the Internet. Other browsers include Lynx, Mosaic and Internet Explorer.

Newsgroup A discussion group on Usenet that focuses on a particular subject.

Off-line The opposite to online, meaning not connected to the Internet.

One-to-one marketing Also known as mass customisation, refers to a type of marketing which involves highly targeted and individually tailored marketing messages. The Internet is well suited to this type of marketing.

Outernet The range of on-line subscription services and databases which are accessible via the Internet.

PGP Pretty Good Privacy, an encryption program used to encode e-mail messages and files.

Post Send a message to a Usenet Newsgroup.

Push Push, or Web broadcasting as it is also known, enables users to have information which matches a predefined set of criteria delivered to their desktops directly without having to go out and seek it.

Relationship marketing A type of marketing which involves maintaining a dialogue with stakeholders - a process which then translates into customer loyalty. This type of marketing is suited to the Internet because of its interactive abilities.

Routers Devices that transfer (route) data between LANs using any form of connection technology. They often work in pairs, one each side of the connection. A router will always be needed to access the Internet - either between an organisation's LAN and a Leased Line, or between an ISP's dial-in modems and *their* LAN. The latter is the case for standard, stand-alone Internet access via a modem (or ISDN-TA). The modems 'extend' the ISP's router, which treats the customer as a LAN of only a single computer.

Search engines These are databases of Web sites which you can search via the Web using key words. They are used for finding information on the Internet.

Server A computer that shares data with and controls its flow to other computers on a network.

SET (Secure Electronic Transaction) A protocol and a standard designed for handling credit-card transactions over the Internet.

SSL (Secure Sockets Layer) A protocol which provides authentication, confidentiality and integrity of data communications between a Web Server and Browser.

Shareware Try-before-you-buy software. Programs that are made available, often via the Internet, for free evaluation for a specific time period, after which, if satisfied, you are required to pay a registration fee.

Signature A few lines of text, usually added automatically, to any e-mail message you post. It should include your name, organisation, address, telephone and fax numbers, and e-mail address.

Spam To post the same message to many and/or inappropriate Newsgroups. An online version of junk mail that causes annoyance and creates an unprofessional image.

UNIX A common computer operating system used on many computer networks that are linked to the Internet.

URL Uniform Resource Locator, a standard method for describing Internet addresses.

Usenet A huge group of computer systems that exchange discussions on thousands of topics called Newsgroups. Effectively a global messaging or bulletin board system.

Value added marketing A type of marketing which focuses on giving something of value to the consumer in exchange for listening to a marketing message. On the Internet, this is typically information, entertainment or something supplied free of charge.

Wide Area Networks The linking of two or more LANs within the same organisation but between geographically separate locations. These connections are much more expensive than LAN cabling, and are usually ISDN or Leased Lines (although modems are possible). Bandwidths range from 64Kbps to 34Mbps+

World Wide Web/WWW/Web A hypertext-based system for storing and retrieving information, enabling text, graphics, sound and video to be presented on screen. Other resources can be accessed via hypertext links.

Zip A common file format for compressing computer files, usually created using the PKZIP program. Files available via the Internet are often stored in this compressed format. Such files will have the .zip suffix, eg. filename.zip.

Index

OPEN ME NOW! *Herschell Gordon Lewis*

Every year, half a billion pieces of worthwhile direct mail are tossed into the wastebasket because whoever designed their envelopes didn't know how to convince the recipient to **Open Me Now!** Did you know that putting nothing on the envelope except a provocative return address can pull a better response than extensive full-colour treatment? Did you know that using a PO Box as a return address can hurt response? You'll find out why in this tightly written no-nonsense guide to envelope use.

Size 6x9 ins 136 pages Retail Price: £36.50

HOW TO CREATE POWERFUL NEWSLETTERS *Peggy Nelson*

Newsletters are a vital resource to organisation communications. But what makes certain newsletters work and others flat and pointless? This book gives you the can't-miss keys to newsletter success that will ensure a reader-enticing blend of information.

Size 7x10 ins 210 pages Retail Price: £27.50

SILVER LININGS *Herschell Gordon Lewis*

Selling to the expanding mature market - the mature (over 55) market place is not only the fastest-growing market segment in the world today. It's also one of the most misunderstood. This book does more than explode the myths of this mammoth marketplace. It delivers hard rules for advertising to the only age group whose numbers will take a quantum leap in the first quarter of the 21st century. For the serious marketer, this new book by Herschell Gordon Lewis is an absolute *must*.

Size 6x9 ins 165 pages Retail Price: £36.50

All titles available from:

Gazelle Book Services
129 Leighton Gdns, London NW10 3PS
Tel: 0181-960 7918 Fax: 0171-794 8609

BONUS BOOKS FOR MARKETING